Cymbeline by William Shakespeare

The life of William Shakespeare, arguably the most significant figure in the Western literary canon, is relatively unknown.

Shakespeare was born in Stratford-upon-Avon in 1565, possibly on the 23rd April, St. George's Day, and baptised there on 26th April.

Little is known of his education and the first firm facts to his life relate to his marriage, aged 18, to Anne Hathaway, who was 26 and from the nearby village of Shottery. Anne gave birth to their first son six months later.

Shakespeare's first play, The Comedy of Errors began a procession of real heavyweights that were to emanate from his pen in a career of just over twenty years in which 37 plays were written and his reputation forever established.

This early skill was recognised by many and by 1594 the Lord Chamberlain's Men were performing his works. With the advantage of Shakespeare's progressive writing they rapidly became London's leading company of players, affording him more exposure and, following the death of Queen Elizabeth in 1603, a royal patent by the new king, James I, at which point they changed their name to the King's Men.

By 1598, and despite efforts to pirate his work, Shakespeare's name was well known and had become a selling point in its own right on title pages.

No plays are attributed to Shakespeare after 1613, and the last few plays he wrote before this time were in collaboration with other writers, one of whom is likely to be John Fletcher who succeeded him as the house playwright for the King's Men.

William Shakespeare died two months later on April 23rd, 1616, survived by his wife, two daughters and a legacy of writing that none have since yet eclipsed.

Index Of Contents
DRAMATIS PERSONAE
ACT I
Scene I - Britain. The Garden of Cymbeline's Palace.
Scene II - The Same. A Public Place.
Scene III - A Room in Cymbeline's Palace.
Scene IV - Rome. Philario's House.
Scene V - Britain. A Room in Cymbeline's Palace.
Scene VI - The Same. Another Room in the Palace.
ACT II
Scene I - Britain. Before Cymbeline's Palace.
Scene II - Imogen's Bedchamber in Cymbeline's Palace:
Scene IV - Rome. Philario's house.
Scene V - Another room in Philario's House.
ACT III
Scene I - Britain. A Hall in Cymbeline's Palace.

Scene II - Another Room in the Palace.
Scene III - Wales: a Mountainous Country with a Cave.
Scene IV - Country Near Milford-Haven.
Scene V - A Room in Cymbeline's Palace.
Scene VI - Wales. Before the Cave of Belarius.
Scene VII - Rome. A Public Place.
ACT IV
Scene I - Wales: Near the Cave of Belarius.
Scene II - Before the Cave of Belarius.
Scene III - A Room in Cymbeline's Palace.
Scene IV - Wales: Before the Cave of Belarius.
ACT V
Scene I - Britain. The Roman Camp.
Scene II - Field of Battle Between the British and Roman Camps.
Scene III - Another Part of the Field.
Scene IV - A British Prison.
Scene V - Cymbeline's Tent.
William Shakespeare – A Short Biography
William Shakespeare – A Concise Bibliography
Shakespeare; or, the Poet by Ralph Waldo Emerson
William Shakespeare – A Tribute in Verse

DRAMATIS PERSONAE
CYMBELINE, King of Britain
CLOTEN, son to the Queen by a former husband
POSTHUMUS LEONATUS, a gentleman, husband to Imogen
BELARIUS, a banished Lord, disguised under the name of Morgan
GUIDERIUS, ARVIRAGUS, sons to Cymbeline, supposed sons to Morgan
PHILARIO, friend to Posthumus
IACHIMO, friend to Philario
A French Gentleman, friend to Philario
CAIUS LUCIUS, general of the Roman forces
A Roman Captain
Two British Captains
PISANIO, servant to Posthumus
CORNELIUS, a physician
Two Lords of Cymbeline's Court
Two Gentlemen of the same
Two Gaolers
QUEEN, wife to Cymbeline
IMOGEN, daughter to Cymbeline by a former Queen
HELEN, a Lady attending on Imogen
Lords, Ladies, Roman Senators, Tribunes, A Dutch Gentleman, A Spanish Gentleman, A Soothsayer, Musicians, Officers, Captains, Soldiers, Messengers, and other Attendants, Apparitions

SCENE—Sometimes in Britain, Sometimes in Italy.

ACT I

SCENE I. Britain. The Garden of Cymbeline's Palace.

Enter two GENTLEMEN

FIRST GENTLEMAN
You do not meet a man but frowns: our bloods
No more obey the heavens than our courtiers
Still seem as does the king.

SECOND GENTLEMAN
But what's the matter?

FIRST GENTLEMAN
His daughter, and the heir of's kingdom, whom
He purposed to his wife's sole son—a widow
That late he married—hath referr'd herself
Unto a poor but worthy gentleman: she's wedded;
Her husband banish'd; she imprison'd: all
Is outward sorrow; though I think the king
Be touch'd at very heart.

SECOND GENTLEMAN
None but the king?

FIRST GENTLEMAN
He that hath lost her too; so is the queen,
That most desired the match; but not a courtier,
Although they wear their faces to the bent
Of the king's look's, hath a heart that is not
Glad at the thing they scowl at.

SECOND GENTLEMAN
And why so?

FIRST GENTLEMAN
He that hath miss'd the princess is a thing
Too bad for bad report: and he that hath her—
I mean, that married her, alack, good man!
And therefore banish'd—is a creature such
As, to seek through the regions of the earth
For one his like, there would be something failing
In him that should compare. I do not think
So fair an outward and such stuff within
Endows a man but he.

SECOND GENTLEMAN
You speak him far.

FIRST GENTLEMAN
I do extend him, sir, within himself,
Crush him together rather than unfold
His measure duly.

SECOND GENTLEMAN
What's his name and birth?

FIRST GENTLEMAN
I cannot delve him to the root: his father
Was call'd Sicilius, who did join his honour
Against the Romans with Cassibelan,
But had his titles by Tenantius whom
He served with glory and admired success,
So gain'd the sur-addition Leonatus;
And had, besides this gentleman in question,
Two other sons, who in the wars o' the time
Died with their swords in hand; for which their father,
Then old and fond of issue, took such sorrow
That he quit being, and his gentle lady,
Big of this gentleman our theme, deceased
As he was born. The king he takes the babe
To his protection, calls him Posthumus Leonatus,
Breeds him and makes him of his bed-chamber,
Puts to him all the learnings that his time
Could make him the receiver of; which he took,
As we do air, fast as 'twas minister'd,
And in's spring became a harvest, lived in court—
Which rare it is to do—most praised, most loved,
A sample to the youngest, to the more mature
A glass that feated them, and to the graver
A child that guided dotards; to his mistress,
For whom he now is banish'd, her own price
Proclaims how she esteem'd him and his virtue;
By her election may be truly read
What kind of man he is.

SECOND GENTLEMAN
I honour him
Even out of your report. But, pray you, tell me,
Is she sole child to the king?

FIRST GENTLEMAN
His only child.
He had two sons: if this be worth your hearing,
Mark it: the eldest of them at three years old,
I' the swathing-clothes the other, from their nursery
Were stol'n, and to this hour no guess in knowledge
Which way they went.

SECOND GENTLEMAN
How long is this ago?

FIRST GENTLEMAN
Some twenty years.

SECOND GENTLEMAN
That a king's children should be so convey'd,
So slackly guarded, and the search so slow,
That could not trace them!

FIRST GENTLEMAN
Howsoe'er 'tis strange,
Or that the negligence may well be laugh'd at,
Yet is it true, sir.

SECOND GENTLEMAN
I do well believe you.

FIRST GENTLEMAN
We must forbear: here comes the gentleman,
The queen, and princess.

Exeunt

Enter the QUEEN, POSTHUMUS LEONATUS, and IMOGEN

QUEEN
No, be assured you shall not find me, daughter,
After the slander of most stepmothers,
Evil-eyed unto you: you're my prisoner, but
Your gaoler shall deliver you the keys
That lock up your restraint. For you, Posthumus,
So soon as I can win the offended king,
I will be known your advocate: marry, yet
The fire of rage is in him, and 'twere good
You lean'd unto his sentence with what patience
Your wisdom may inform you.

POSTHUMUS LEONATUS
Please your highness,
I will from hence to-day.

QUEEN
You know the peril.
I'll fetch a turn about the garden, pitying
The pangs of barr'd affections, though the king
Hath charged you should not speak together.

Exit

IMOGEN
O Dissembling courtesy! How fine this tyrant
Can tickle where she wounds! My dearest husband,
I something fear my father's wrath; but nothing—
Always reserved my holy duty—what
His rage can do on me: you must be gone;
And I shall here abide the hourly shot
Of angry eyes, not comforted to live,
But that there is this jewel in the world
That I may see again.

POSTHUMUS LEONATUS
My queen! my mistress!
O lady, weep no more, lest I give cause
To be suspected of more tenderness
Than doth become a man. I will remain
The loyal'st husband that did e'er plight troth:
My residence in Rome at one Philario's,
Who to my father was a friend, to me
Known but by letter: thither write, my queen,
And with mine eyes I'll drink the words you send,
Though ink be made of gall.

Re-enter QUEEN

QUEEN
Be brief, I pray you:
If the king come, I shall incur I know not
How much of his displeasure.

Aside

Yet I'll move him
To walk this way: I never do him wrong,
But he does buy my injuries, to be friends;
Pays dear for my offences.

Exit

POSTHUMUS LEONATUS
Should we be taking leave
As long a term as yet we have to live,
The loathness to depart would grow. Adieu!

IMOGEN
Nay, stay a little:
Were you but riding forth to air yourself,
Such parting were too petty. Look here, love;
This diamond was my mother's: take it, heart;
But keep it till you woo another wife,
When Imogen is dead.

POSTHUMUS LEONATUS
How, how! another?
You gentle gods, give me but this I have,
And sear up my embracements from a next
With bonds of death!

Putting on the ring

Remain, remain thou here
While sense can keep it on. And, sweetest, fairest,
As I my poor self did exchange for you,
To your so infinite loss, so in our trifles
I still win of you: for my sake wear this;
It is a manacle of love; I'll place it
Upon this fairest prisoner.

Putting a bracelet upon her arm

IMOGEN
O the gods!
When shall we see again?

Enter CYMBELINE and Lords

POSTHUMUS LEONATUS
Alack, the king!

CYMBELINE
Thou basest thing, avoid! hence, from my sight!
If after this command thou fraught the court
With thy unworthiness, thou diest: away!
Thou'rt poison to my blood.

POSTHUMUS LEONATUS
The gods protect you!
And bless the good remainders of the court! I am gone.

Exit

IMOGEN
There cannot be a pinch in death
More sharp than this is.

CYMBELINE
O disloyal thing,
That shouldst repair my youth, thou heap'st
A year's age on me.

IMOGEN

I beseech you, sir,
Harm not yourself with your vexation
I am senseless of your wrath; a touch more rare
Subdues all pangs, all fears.

CYMBELINE
Past grace? obedience?

IMOGEN
Past hope, and in despair; that way, past grace.

CYMBELINE
That mightst have had the sole son of my queen!

IMOGEN
O blest, that I might not! I chose an eagle,
And did avoid a puttock.

CYMBELINE
Thou took'st a beggar; wouldst have made my throne
A seat for baseness.

IMOGEN
No; I rather added
A lustre to it.

CYMBELINE
O thou vile one!

IMOGEN
Sir,
It is your fault that I have loved Posthumus:
You bred him as my playfellow, and he is
A man worth any woman, overbuys me
Almost the sum he pays.

CYMBELINE
What, art thou mad?

IMOGEN
Almost, sir: heaven restore me! Would I were
A neat-herd's daughter, and my Leonatus
Our neighbour shepherd's son!

CYMBELINE
Thou foolish thing!

Re-enter QUEEN

They were again together: you have done
Not after our command. Away with her,
And pen her up.

QUEEN
Beseech your patience. Peace,
Dear lady daughter, peace! Sweet sovereign,
Leave us to ourselves; and make yourself some comfort
Out of your best advice.

CYMBELINE
Nay, let her languish
A drop of blood a day; and, being aged,
Die of this folly!

Exeunt CYMBELINE and Lords

QUEEN
Fie! you must give way.

Enter PISANIO

Here is your servant. How now, sir! What news?

PISANIO
My lord your son drew on my master.

QUEEN
Ha!
No harm, I trust, is done?

PISANIO
There might have been,
But that my master rather play'd than fought
And had no help of anger: they were parted
By gentlemen at hand.

QUEEN
I am very glad on't.

IMOGEN
Your son's my father's friend; he takes his part.
To draw upon an exile! O brave sir!
I would they were in Afric both together;
Myself by with a needle, that I might prick
The goer-back. Why came you from your master?

PISANIO
On his command: he would not suffer me
To bring him to the haven; left these notes

Of what commands I should be subject to,
When 't pleased you to employ me.

QUEEN
This hath been
Your faithful servant: I dare lay mine honour
He will remain so.

PISANIO
I humbly thank your highness.

QUEEN
Pray, walk awhile.

IMOGEN
About some half-hour hence,
I pray you, speak with me: you shall at least
Go see my lord aboard: for this time leave me.

Exeunt

SCENE II. The Same. A Public Place.

Enter CLOTEN and two LORDS

FIRST LORD
Sir, I would advise you to shift a shirt; the violence of action hath made you reek as a sacrifice: where air comes out, air comes in: there's none abroad so wholesome as that you vent.

CLOTEN
If my shirt were bloody, then to shift it. Have I hurt him?

SECOND LORD
[Aside] No, 'faith; not so much as his patience.

FIRST LORD
Hurt him! his body's a passable carcass, if he be not hurt: it is a thoroughfare for steel, if it be not hurt.

SECOND LORD
[Aside] His steel was in debt; it went o' the backside the town.

CLOTEN
The villain would not stand me.

SECOND LORD
[Aside] No; but he fled forward still, toward your face.

FIRST LORD

Stand you! You have land enough of your own: but he added to your having; gave you some ground.

SECOND LORD
[Aside] As many inches as you have oceans. Puppies!

CLOTEN
I would they had not come between us.

SECOND LORD
[Aside] So would I, till you had measured how long a fool you were upon the ground.

CLOTEN
And that she should love this fellow and refuse me!

SECOND LORD
[Aside] If it be a sin to make a true election, she is damned.

FIRST LORD
Sir, as I told you always, her beauty and her brain go not together: she's a good sign, but I have seen small reflection of her wit.

SECOND LORD
[Aside] She shines not upon fools, lest the reflection should hurt her.

CLOTEN
Come, I'll to my chamber. Would there had been some hurt done!

SECOND LORD
[Aside] I wish not so; unless it had been the fall of an ass, which is no great hurt.

CLOTEN
You'll go with us?

FIRST LORD
I'll attend your lordship.

CLOTEN
Nay, come, let's go together.

SECOND LORD
Well, my lord.

Exeunt

SCENE III. A Room in Cymbeline's Palace.

Enter IMOGEN and PISANIO

IMOGEN

I would thou grew'st unto the shores o' the haven,
And question'dst every sail: if he should write
And not have it, 'twere a paper lost,
As offer'd mercy is. What was the last
That he spake to thee?

PISANIO
It was his queen, his queen!

IMOGEN
Then waved his handkerchief?

PISANIO
And kiss'd it, madam.

IMOGEN
Senseless Linen! happier therein than I!
And that was all?

PISANIO
No, madam; for so long
As he could make me with this eye or ear
Distinguish him from others, he did keep
The deck, with glove, or hat, or handkerchief,
Still waving, as the fits and stirs of 's mind
Could best express how slow his soul sail'd on,
How swift his ship.

IMOGEN
Thou shouldst have made him
As little as a crow, or less, ere left
To after-eye him.

PISANIO
Madam, so I did.

IMOGEN
I would have broke mine eye-strings; crack'd them, but
To look upon him, till the diminution
Of space had pointed him sharp as my needle,
Nay, follow'd him, till he had melted from
The smallness of a gnat to air, and then
Have turn'd mine eye and wept. But, good Pisanio,
When shall we hear from him?

PISANIO
Be assured, madam,
With his next vantage.

IMOGEN

I did not take my leave of him, but had
Most pretty things to say: ere I could tell him
How I would think on him at certain hours
Such thoughts and such, or I could make him swear
The shes of Italy should not betray
Mine interest and his honour, or have charged him,
At the sixth hour of morn, at noon, at midnight,
To encounter me with orisons, for then
I am in heaven for him; or ere I could
Give him that parting kiss which I had set
Betwixt two charming words, comes in my father
And like the tyrannous breathing of the north
Shakes all our buds from growing.

Enter a LADY

LADY
The queen, madam,
Desires your highness' company.

IMOGEN
Those things I bid you do, get them dispatch'd.
I will attend the queen.

PISANIO
Madam, I shall.

Exeunt

SCENE IV. Rome. Philario's House.

Enter PHILARIO, IACHIMO, a FRENCHMAN, a DUTCHMAN, and a SPANIARD

IACHIMO
Believe it, sir, I have seen him in Britain: he was then of a crescent note, expected to prove so worthy as since he hath been allowed the name of; but I could then have looked on him without the help of admiration, though the catalogue of his endowments had been tabled by his side and I to peruse him by items.

PHILARIO
You speak of him when he was less furnished than now he is with that which makes him both without and within.

FRENCHMAN
I have seen him in France: we had very many there could behold the sun with as firm eyes as he.

IACHIMO
This matter of marrying his king's daughter, wherein he must be weighed rather by her value than his own, words him, I doubt not, a great deal from the matter.

FRENCHMAN
And then his banishment.

IACHIMO
Ay, and the approbation of those that weep this lamentable divorce under her colours are wonderfully to extend him; be it but to fortify her judgment, which else an easy battery might lay flat, for taking a beggar without less quality. But how comes it he is to sojourn with you? How creeps acquaintance?

PHILARIO
His father and I were soldiers together; to whom I have been often bound for no less than my life. Here comes the Briton: let him be so entertained amongst you as suits, with gentlemen of your knowing, to a stranger of his quality.

Enter POSTHUMUS LEONATUS

I beseech you all, be better known to this gentleman; whom I commend to you as a noble friend of mine: how worthy he is I will leave to appear hereafter, rather than story him in his own hearing.

FRENCHMAN
Sir, we have known together in Orleans.

POSTHUMUS LEONATUS
Since when I have been debtor to you for courtesies, which I will be ever to pay and yet pay still.

FRENCHMAN
Sir, you o'er-rate my poor kindness: I was glad I did atone my countryman and you; it had been pity you should have been put together with so mortal a purpose as then each bore, upon importance of so slight and trivial a nature.

POSTHUMUS LEONATUS
By your pardon, sir, I was then a young traveller; rather shunned to go even with what I heard than in my every action to be guided by others' experiences: but upon my mended judgment—if I offend not to say it is mended—my quarrel was not altogether slight.

FRENCHMAN
'Faith, yes, to be put to the arbitrement of swords, and by such two that would by all likelihood have confounded one the other, or have fallen both.

IACHIMO
Can we, with manners, ask what was the difference?

FRENCHMAN
Safely, I think: 'twas a contention in public, which may, without contradiction, suffer the report. It was much like an argument that fell out last night, where each of us fell in praise of our country mistresses; this gentleman at that time vouching—and upon warrant of bloody affirmation—his to be more fair, virtuous, wise, chaste, constant-qualified and less attemptable than any the rarest of our ladies in France.

IACHIMO

That lady is not now living, or this gentleman's opinion by this worn out.

POSTHUMUS LEONATUS
She holds her virtue still and I my mind.

IACHIMO
You must not so far prefer her 'fore ours of Italy.

POSTHUMUS LEONATUS
Being so far provoked as I was in France, I would abate her nothing, though I profess myself her adorer, not her friend.

IACHIMO
As fair and as good—a kind of hand-in-hand comparison—had been something too fair and too good for any lady in Britain. If she went before others I have seen, as that diamond of yours outlustres many I have beheld. I could not but believe she excelled many: but I have not seen the most precious diamond that is, nor you the lady.

POSTHUMUS LEONATUS
I praised her as I rated her: so do I my stone.

IACHIMO
What do you esteem it at?

POSTHUMUS LEONATUS
More than the world enjoys.

IACHIMO
Either your unparagoned mistress is dead, or she's outprized by a trifle.

POSTHUMUS LEONATUS
You are mistaken: the one may be sold, or given, if there were wealth enough for the purchase, or merit for the gift: the other is not a thing for sale, and only the gift of the gods.

IACHIMO
Which the gods have given you?

POSTHUMUS LEONATUS
Which, by their graces, I will keep.

IACHIMO
You may wear her in title yours: but, you know, strange fowl light upon neighbouring ponds. Your ring may be stolen too: so your brace of unprizable estimations; the one is but frail and the other casual; a cunning thief, or a that way accomplished courtier, would hazard the winning both of first and last.

POSTHUMUS LEONATUS
Your Italy contains none so accomplished a courtier to convince the honour of my mistress, if, in the holding or loss of that, you term her frail. I do nothing doubt you have store of thieves; notwithstanding, I fear not my ring.

PHILARIO
Let us leave here, gentlemen.

POSTHUMUS LEONATUS
Sir, with all my heart. This worthy signior, I thank him, makes no stranger of me; we are familiar at first.

IACHIMO
With five times so much conversation, I should get ground of your fair mistress, make her go back, even to the yielding, had I admittance and opportunity to friend.

POSTHUMUS LEONATUS
No, no.

IACHIMO
I dare thereupon pawn the moiety of my estate to your ring; which, in my opinion, o'ervalues it something: but I make my wager rather against your confidence than her reputation: and, to bar your offence herein too, I durst attempt it against any lady in the world.

POSTHUMUS LEONATUS
You are a great deal abused in too bold a persuasion; and I doubt not you sustain what you're worthy of by your attempt.

IACHIMO
What's that?

POSTHUMUS LEONATUS
A repulse: though your attempt, as you call it, deserve more; a punishment too.

PHILARIO
Gentlemen, enough of this: it came in too suddenly; let it die as it was born, and, I pray you, be better acquainted.

IACHIMO
Would I had put my estate and my neighbour's on the approbation of what I have spoke!

POSTHUMUS LEONATUS
What lady would you choose to assail?

IACHIMO
Yours; whom in constancy you think stands so safe. I will lay you ten thousand ducats to your ring, that, commend me to the court where your lady is, with no more advantage than the opportunity of a second conference, and I will bring from thence that honour of hers which you imagine so reserved.

POSTHUMUS LEONATUS
I will wage against your gold, gold to it: my ring I hold dear as my finger; 'tis part of it.

IACHIMO
You are afraid, and therein the wiser. If you buy ladies' flesh at a million a dram, you cannot preserve it from tainting: but I see you have some religion in you, that you fear.

POSTHUMUS LEONATUS
This is but a custom in your tongue; you bear a graver purpose, I hope.

IACHIMO
I am the master of my speeches, and would undergo what's spoken, I swear.

POSTHUMUS LEONATUS
Will you? I shall but lend my diamond till your return: let there be covenants drawn between's: my mistress exceeds in goodness the hugeness of your unworthy thinking: I dare you to this match: here's my ring.

PHILARIO
I will have it no lay.

IACHIMO
By the gods, it is one. If I bring you no sufficient testimony that I have enjoyed the dearest bodily part of your mistress, my ten thousand ducats are yours; so is your diamond too: if I come off, and leave her in such honour as you have trust in, she your jewel, this your jewel, and my gold are yours: provided I have your commendation for my more free entertainment.

POSTHUMUS LEONATUS
I embrace these conditions; let us have articles betwixt us. Only, thus far you shall answer: if you make your voyage upon her and give me directly to understand you have prevailed, I am no further your enemy; she is not worth our debate: if she remain unseduced, you not making it appear otherwise, for your ill opinion and the assault you have made to her chastity you shall answer me with your sword.

IACHIMO
Your hand; a covenant: we will have these things set down by lawful counsel, and straight away for Britain, lest the bargain should catch cold and starve: I will fetch my gold and have our two wagers recorded.

POSTHUMUS LEONATUS
Agreed.

Exeunt POSTHUMUS LEONATUS and IACHIMO

FRENCHMAN
Will this hold, think you?

PHILARIO
Signior Iachimo will not from it.
Pray, let us follow 'em.

Exeunt

SCENE V. Britain. A Room in Cymbeline's Palace.

Enter QUEEN, LADIES, and CORNELIUS

QUEEN
Whiles yet the dew's on ground, gather those flowers;
Make haste: who has the note of them?

FIRST LADY
I, madam.

QUEEN
Dispatch.

Exeunt LADIES

Now, master doctor, have you brought those drugs?

CORNELIUS
Pleaseth your highness, ay: here they are, madam:

Presenting a small box

But I beseech your grace, without offence,—
My conscience bids me ask—wherefore you have
Commanded of me those most poisonous compounds,
Which are the movers of a languishing death;
But though slow, deadly?

QUEEN
I wonder, doctor,
Thou ask'st me such a question. Have I not been
Thy pupil long? Hast thou not learn'd me how
To make perfumes? distil? preserve? yea, so
That our great king himself doth woo me oft
For my confections? Having thus far proceeded,—
Unless thou think'st me devilish—is't not meet
That I did amplify my judgment in
Other conclusions? I will try the forces
Of these thy compounds on such creatures as
We count not worth the hanging, but none human,
To try the vigour of them and apply
Allayments to their act, and by them gather
Their several virtues and effects.

CORNELIUS
Your highness
Shall from this practise but make hard your heart:
Besides, the seeing these effects will be
Both noisome and infectious.

QUEEN
O, content thee.

Enter PISANIO

Aside
Here comes a flattering rascal; upon him
Will I first work: he's for his master,
An enemy to my son. How now, Pisanio!
Doctor, your service for this time is ended;
Take your own way.

CORNELIUS
[Aside] I do suspect you, madam;
But you shall do no harm.

QUEEN
[To PISANIO] Hark thee, a word.

CORNELIUS
[Aside] I do not like her. She doth think she has
Strange lingering poisons: I do know her spirit,
And will not trust one of her malice with
A drug of such damn'd nature. Those she has
Will stupefy and dull the sense awhile;
Which first, perchance, she'll prove on cats and dogs,
Then afterward up higher: but there is
No danger in what show of death it makes,
More than the locking-up the spirits a time,
To be more fresh, reviving. She is fool'd
With a most false effect; and I the truer,
So to be false with her.

QUEEN
No further service, doctor,
Until I send for thee.

CORNELIUS
I humbly take my leave.

Exit

QUEEN
Weeps she still, say'st thou? Dost thou think in time
She will not quench and let instructions enter
Where folly now possesses? Do thou work:
When thou shalt bring me word she loves my son,
I'll tell thee on the instant thou art then
As great as is thy master, greater, for
His fortunes all lie speechless and his name
Is at last gasp: return he cannot, nor
Continue where he is: to shift his being
Is to exchange one misery with another,

And every day that comes comes to decay
A day's work in him. What shalt thou expect,
To be depender on a thing that leans,
Who cannot be new built, nor has no friends,
So much as but to prop him?

The QUEEN drops the box: PISANIO takes it up

Thou takest up
Thou know'st not what; but take it for thy labour:
It is a thing I made, which hath the king
Five times redeem'd from death: I do not know
What is more cordial. Nay, I prethee, take it;
It is an earnest of a further good
That I mean to thee. Tell thy mistress how
The case stands with her; do't as from thyself.
Think what a chance thou changest on, but think
Thou hast thy mistress still, to boot, my son,
Who shall take notice of thee: I'll move the king
To any shape of thy preferment such
As thou'lt desire; and then myself, I chiefly,
That set thee on to this desert, am bound
To load thy merit richly. Call my women:
Think on my words.

Exit PISANIO

A sly and constant knave,
Not to be shaked; the agent for his master
And the remembrancer of her to hold
The hand-fast to her lord. I have given him that
Which, if he take, shall quite unpeople her
Of liegers for her sweet, and which she after,
Except she bend her humour, shall be assured
To taste of too.

Re-enter PISANIO and LADIES

So, so: well done, well done:
The violets, cowslips, and the primroses,
Bear to my closet. Fare thee well, Pisanio;
Think on my words.

Exeunt QUEEN and LADIES

PISANIO
And shall do:
But when to my good lord I prove untrue,
I'll choke myself: there's all I'll do for you.

Exit

SCENE VI. The Same. Another Room in the Palace.

Enter IMOGEN

IMOGEN
A father cruel, and a step-dame false;
A foolish suitor to a wedded lady,
That hath her husband banish'd;—O, that husband!
My supreme crown of grief! and those repeated
Vexations of it! Had I been thief-stol'n,
As my two brothers, happy! but most miserable
Is the desire that's glorious: blest be those,
How mean soe'er, that have their honest wills,
Which seasons comfort. Who may this be? Fie!

Enter PISANIO and IACHIMO

PISANIO
Madam, a noble gentleman of Rome,
Comes from my lord with letters.

IACHIMO
Change you, madam?
The worthy Leonatus is in safety
And greets your highness dearly.

Presents a letter

IMOGEN
Thanks, good sir:
You're kindly welcome.

IACHIMO
[Aside] All of her that is out of door most rich!
If she be furnish'd with a mind so rare,
She is alone the Arabian bird, and I
Have lost the wager. Boldness be my friend!
Arm me, audacity, from head to foot!
Or, like the Parthian, I shall flying fight;
Rather directly fly.

IMOGEN
[Reads] 'He is one of the noblest note, to whose
kindnesses I am most infinitely tied. Reflect upon
him accordingly, as you value your trust—

LEONATUS.'
So far I read aloud:

But even the very middle of my heart
Is warm'd by the rest, and takes it thankfully.
You are as welcome, worthy sir, as I
Have words to bid you, and shall find it so
In all that I can do.

IACHIMO
Thanks, fairest lady.
What, are men mad? Hath nature given them eyes
To see this vaulted arch, and the rich crop
Of sea and land, which can distinguish 'twixt
The fiery orbs above and the twinn'd stones
Upon the number'd beach? and can we not
Partition make with spectacles so precious
'Twixt fair and foul?

IMOGEN
What makes your admiration?

IACHIMO
It cannot be i' the eye, for apes and monkeys
'Twixt two such shes would chatter this way and
Contemn with mows the other; nor i' the judgment,
For idiots in this case of favour would
Be wisely definite; nor i' the appetite;
Sluttery to such neat excellence opposed
Should make desire vomit emptiness,
Not so allured to feed.

IMOGEN
What is the matter, trow?

IACHIMO
The cloyed will,
That satiate yet unsatisfied desire, that tub
Both fill'd and running, ravening first the lamb
Longs after for the garbage.

IMOGEN
What, dear sir,
Thus raps you? Are you well?

IACHIMO
Thanks, madam; well.

To PISANIO

Beseech you, sir, desire
My man's abode where I did leave him: he
Is strange and peevish.

PISANIO
I was going, sir,
To give him welcome.

Exit

IMOGEN
Continues well my lord? His health, beseech you?

IACHIMO
Well, madam.

IMOGEN
Is he disposed to mirth? I hope he is.

IACHIMO
Exceeding pleasant; none a stranger there
So merry and so gamesome: he is call'd
The Briton reveller.

IMOGEN
When he was here,
He did incline to sadness, and oft-times
Not knowing why.

IACHIMO
I never saw him sad.
There is a Frenchman his companion, one
An eminent monsieur, that, it seems, much loves
A Gallian girl at home; he furnaces
The thick sighs from him, whiles the jolly Briton—
Your lord, I mean—laughs from's free lungs, cries 'O,
Can my sides hold, to think that man, who knows
By history, report, or his own proof,
What woman is, yea, what she cannot choose
But must be, will his free hours languish for
Assured bondage?'

IMOGEN
Will my lord say so?

IACHIMO
Ay, madam, with his eyes in flood with laughter:
It is a recreation to be by
And hear him mock the Frenchman. But, heavens know,
Some men are much to blame.

IMOGEN
Not he, I hope.

IACHIMO

Not he: but yet heaven's bounty towards him might
Be used more thankfully. In himself, 'tis much;
In you, which I account his beyond all talents,
Whilst I am bound to wonder, I am bound
To pity too.

IMOGEN
What do you pity, sir?

IACHIMO
Two creatures heartily.

IMOGEN
Am I one, sir?
You look on me: what wreck discern you in me
Deserves your pity?

IACHIMO
Lamentable! What,
To hide me from the radiant sun and solace
I' the dungeon by a snuff?

IMOGEN
I pray you, sir,
Deliver with more openness your answers
To my demands. Why do you pity me?

IACHIMO
That others do—
I was about to say—enjoy your—But
It is an office of the gods to venge it,
Not mine to speak on 't.

IMOGEN
You do seem to know
Something of me, or what concerns me: pray you,—
Since doubling things go ill often hurts more
Than to be sure they do; for certainties
Either are past remedies, or, timely knowing,
The remedy then born—discover to me
What both you spur and stop.

IACHIMO
Had I this cheek
To bathe my lips upon; this hand, whose touch,
Whose every touch, would force the feeler's soul
To the oath of loyalty; this object, which
Takes prisoner the wild motion of mine eye,
Fixing it only here; should I, damn'd then,
Slaver with lips as common as the stairs
That mount the Capitol; join gripes with hands

Made hard with hourly falsehood—falsehood, as
With labour; then by-peeping in an eye
Base and unlustrous as the smoky light
That's fed with stinking tallow; it were fit
That all the plagues of hell should at one time
Encounter such revolt.

IMOGEN
My lord, I fear,
Has forgot Britain.

IACHIMO
And himself. Not I,
Inclined to this intelligence, pronounce
The beggary of his change; but 'tis your graces
That from pay mutest conscience to my tongue
Charms this report out.

IMOGEN
Let me hear no more.

IACHIMO
O dearest soul! your cause doth strike my heart
With pity, that doth make me sick. A lady
So fair, and fasten'd to an empery,
Would make the great'st king double,—to be partner'd
With tomboys hired with that self-exhibition
Which your own coffers yield! with diseased ventures
That play with all infirmities for gold
Which rottenness can lend nature! such boil'd stuff
As well might poison poison! Be revenged;
Or she that bore you was no queen, and you
Recoil from your great stock.

IMOGEN
Revenged!
How should I be revenged? If this be true,—
As I have such a heart that both mine ears
Must not in haste abuse—if it be true,
How should I be revenged?

IACHIMO
Should he make me
Live, like Diana's priest, betwixt cold sheets,
Whiles he is vaulting variable ramps,
In your despite, upon your purse? Revenge it.
I dedicate myself to your sweet pleasure,
More noble than that runagate to your bed,
And will continue fast to your affection,
Still close as sure.

IMOGEN
What, ho, Pisanio!

IACHIMO
Let me my service tender on your lips.

IMOGEN
Away! I do condemn mine ears that have
So long attended thee. If thou wert honourable,
Thou wouldst have told this tale for virtue, not
For such an end thou seek'st,—as base as strange.
Thou wrong'st a gentleman, who is as far
From thy report as thou from honour, and
Solicit'st here a lady that disdains
Thee and the devil alike. What ho, Pisanio!
The king my father shall be made acquainted
Of thy assault: if he shall think it fit,
A saucy stranger in his court to mart
As in a Romish stew and to expound
His beastly mind to us, he hath a court
He little cares for and a daughter who
He not respects at all. What, ho, Pisanio!

IACHIMO
O happy Leonatus! I may say
The credit that thy lady hath of thee
Deserves thy trust, and thy most perfect goodness
Her assured credit. Blessed live you long!
A lady to the worthiest sir that ever
Country call'd his! and you his mistress, only
For the most worthiest fit! Give me your pardon.
I have spoke this, to know if your affiance
Were deeply rooted; and shall make your lord,
That which he is, new o'er: and he is one
The truest manner'd; such a holy witch
That he enchants societies into him;
Half all men's hearts are his.

IMOGEN
You make amends.

IACHIMO
He sits 'mongst men like a descended god:
He hath a kind of honour sets him off,
More than a mortal seeming. Be not angry,
Most mighty princess, that I have adventured
To try your taking a false report; which hath
Honour'd with confirmation your great judgment
In the election of a sir so rare,
Which you know cannot err: the love I bear him

Made me to fan you thus, but the gods made you,
Unlike all others, chaffless. Pray, your pardon.

IMOGEN
All's well, sir: take my power i' the court
for yours.

IACHIMO
My humble thanks. I had almost forgot
To entreat your grace but in a small request,
And yet of moment to, for it concerns
Your lord; myself and other noble friends,
Are partners in the business.

IMOGEN
Pray, what is't?

IACHIMO
Some dozen Romans of us and your lord—
The best feather of our wing—have mingled sums
To buy a present for the emperor
Which I, the factor for the rest, have done
In France: 'tis plate of rare device, and jewels
Of rich and exquisite form; their values great;
And I am something curious, being strange,
To have them in safe stowage: may it please you
To take them in protection?

IMOGEN
Willingly;
And pawn mine honour for their safety: since
My lord hath interest in them, I will keep them
In my bedchamber.

IACHIMO
They are in a trunk,
Attended by my men: I will make bold
To send them to you, only for this night;
I must aboard to-morrow.

IMOGEN
O, no, no.

IACHIMO
Yes, I beseech; or I shall short my word
By lengthening my return. From Gallia
I cross'd the seas on purpose and on promise
To see your grace.

IMOGEN

I thank you for your pains:
But not away to-morrow!

IACHIMO
O, I must, madam:
Therefore I shall beseech you, if you please
To greet your lord with writing, do't to-night:
I have outstood my time; which is material
To the tender of our present.

IMOGEN
I will write.
Send your trunk to me; it shall safe be kept,
And truly yielded you. You're very welcome.

Exeunt

ACT II

SCENE I. Britain. Before Cymbeline's Palace.

Enter CLOTEN and two LORDS

CLOTEN
Was there ever man had such luck! when I kissed the jack, upon an up-cast to be hit away! I had a hundred pound on't: and then a whoreson jackanapes must take me up for swearing; as if I borrowed mine oaths of him and might not spend them at my pleasure.

FIRST LORD
What got he by that? You have broke his pate with your bowl.

SECOND LORD
[Aside] If his wit had been like him that broke it, it would have run all out.

CLOTEN
When a gentleman is disposed to swear, it is not for any standers-by to curtail his oaths, ha?

SECOND LORD
No my lord;
Aside
nor crop the ears of them.

CLOTEN
Whoreson dog! I give him satisfaction?
Would he had been one of my rank!

SECOND LORD
[Aside] To have smelt like a fool.

CLOTEN
I am not vexed more at any thing in the earth: a pox on't! I had rather not be so noble as I am; they dare not fight with me, because of the queen my mother: every Jack-slave hath his bellyful of fighting, and I must go up and down like a cock that nobody can match.

SECOND LORD
[Aside] You are cock and capon too; and you crow, cock, with your comb on.

CLOTEN
Sayest thou?

SECOND LORD
It is not fit your lordship should undertake every companion that you give offence to.

CLOTEN
No, I know that: but it is fit I should commit offence to my inferiors.

SECOND LORD
Ay, it is fit for your lordship only.

CLOTEN
Why, so I say.

FIRST LORD
Did you hear of a stranger that's come to court to-night?

CLOTEN
A stranger, and I not know on't!

SECOND LORD
[Aside] He's a strange fellow himself, and knows it not.

FIRST LORD
There's an Italian come; and, 'tis thought, one of Leonatus' friends.

CLOTEN
Leonatus! a banished rascal; and he's another, whatsoever he be. Who told you of this stranger?

FIRST LORD
One of your lordship's pages.

CLOTEN
Is it fit I went to look upon him? is there no derogation in't?

SECOND LORD
You cannot derogate, my lord.

CLOTEN
Not easily, I think.

SECOND LORD

[Aside] You are a fool granted; therefore your issues, being foolish, do not derogate.

CLOTEN
Come, I'll go see this Italian: what I have lost to-day at bowls I'll win to-night of him. Come, go.

SECOND LORD
I'll attend your lordship.

Exeunt CLOTEN and FIRST LORD

That such a crafty devil as is his mother
Should yield the world this ass! a woman that
Bears all down with her brain; and this her son
Cannot take two from twenty, for his heart,
And leave eighteen. Alas, poor princess,
Thou divine Imogen, what thou endurest,
Betwixt a father by thy step-dame govern'd,
A mother hourly coining plots, a wooer
More hateful than the foul expulsion is
Of thy dear husband, than that horrid act
Of the divorce he'ld make! The heavens hold firm
The walls of thy dear honour, keep unshaked
That temple, thy fair mind, that thou mayst stand,
To enjoy thy banish'd lord and this great land!

Exit

SCENE II. Imogen's Bedchamber in Cymbeline's Palace:

A trunk in one corner of it.

IMOGEN in bed, reading; a LADY attending

IMOGEN
Who's there? my woman Helen?

LADY
Please you, madam

IMOGEN
What hour is it?

LADY
Almost midnight, madam.

IMOGEN
I have read three hours then: mine eyes are weak:
Fold down the leaf where I have left: to bed:
Take not away the taper, leave it burning;

And if thou canst awake by four o' the clock,
I prithee, call me. Sleep hath seized me wholly

Exit LADY

To your protection I commend me, gods.
From fairies and the tempters of the night
Guard me, beseech ye.

Sleeps.

IACHIMO comes from the trunk

IACHIMO
The crickets sing, and man's o'er-labour'd sense
Repairs itself by rest. Our Tarquin thus
Did softly press the rushes, ere he waken'd
The chastity he wounded. Cytherea,
How bravely thou becomest thy bed, fresh lily,
And whiter than the sheets! That I might touch!
But kiss; one kiss! Rubies unparagon'd,
How dearly they do't! 'Tis her breathing that
Perfumes the chamber thus: the flame o' the taper
Bows toward her, and would under-peep her lids,
To see the enclosed lights, now canopied
Under these windows, white and azure laced
With blue of heaven's own tinct. But my design,
To note the chamber: I will write all down:
Such and such pictures; there the window; such
The adornment of her bed; the arras; figures,
Why, such and such; and the contents o' the story.
Ah, but some natural notes about her body,
Above ten thousand meaner moveables
Would testify, to enrich mine inventory.
O sleep, thou ape of death, lie dull upon her!
And be her sense but as a monument,
Thus in a chapel lying! Come off, come off:

Taking off her bracelet

As slippery as the Gordian knot was hard!
'Tis mine; and this will witness outwardly,
As strongly as the conscience does within,
To the madding of her lord. On her left breast
A mole cinque-spotted, like the crimson drops
I' the bottom of a cowslip: here's a voucher,
Stronger than ever law could make: this secret
Will force him think I have pick'd the lock and ta'en
The treasure of her honour. No more. To what end?
Why should I write this down, that's riveted,
Screw'd to my memory? She hath been reading late

The tale of Tereus; here the leaf's turn'd down
Where Philomel gave up. I have enough:
To the trunk again, and shut the spring of it.
Swift, swift, you dragons of the night, that dawning
May bare the raven's eye! I lodge in fear;
Though this a heavenly angel, hell is here.

Clock strikes

One, two, three: time, time!

Goes into the trunk. The scene closes

Scene III

An ante-chamber adjoining Imogen's apartments.

Enter CLOTEN and Lords

FIRST LORD
Your lordship is the most patient man in loss, the most coldest that ever turned up ace.

CLOTEN
It would make any man cold to lose.

FIRST LORD
But not every man patient after the noble temper of your lordship. You are most hot and furious when you win.

CLOTEN
Winning will put any man into courage. If I could get this foolish Imogen, I should have gold enough. It's almost morning, is't not?

FIRST LORD
Day, my lord.

CLOTEN
I would this music would come: I am advised to give her music o' mornings; they say it will penetrate.

Enter MUSICIANS

Come on; tune: if you can penetrate her with your fingering, so; we'll try with tongue too: if none will do, let her remain; but I'll never give o'er. First, a very excellent good-conceited thing; after, a wonderful sweet air, with admirable rich words to it: and then let her consider.

SONG

Hark, hark! the lark at heaven's gate sings,
And Phoebus 'gins arise,
His steeds to water at those springs
On chaliced flowers that lies;
And winking Mary-buds begin
To ope their golden eyes:
With every thing that pretty is,
My lady sweet, arise:
Arise, arise.

CLOTEN
So, get you gone. If this penetrate, I will consider your music the better: if it do not, it is a vice in her ears, which horse-hairs and calves'-guts, nor the voice of unpaved eunuch to boot, can never amend.

Exeunt MUSICIANS

SECOND LORD
Here comes the king.

CLOTEN
I am glad I was up so late; for that's the reason I was up so early: he cannot choose but take this service I have done fatherly.

Enter CYMBELINE and QUEEN

Good morrow to your majesty and to my gracious mother.

CYMBELINE
Attend you here the door of our stern daughter?
Will she not forth?

CLOTEN
I have assailed her with music, but she vouchsafes no notice.

CYMBELINE
The exile of her minion is too new;
She hath not yet forgot him: some more time
Must wear the print of his remembrance out,
And then she's yours.

QUEEN
You are most bound to the king,
Who lets go by no vantages that may
Prefer you to his daughter. Frame yourself
To orderly soliciting, and be friended
With aptness of the season; make denials
Increase your services; so seem as if
You were inspired to do those duties which
You tender to her; that you in all obey her,
Save when command to your dismission tends,
And therein you are senseless.

CLOTEN
Senseless! not so.

Enter a MESSENGER

MESSENGER
So like you, sir, ambassadors from Rome;
The one is Caius Lucius.

CYMBELINE
A worthy fellow,
Albeit he comes on angry purpose now;
But that's no fault of his: we must receive him
According to the honour of his sender;
And towards himself, his goodness forespent on us,
We must extend our notice. Our dear son,
When you have given good morning to your mistress,
Attend the queen and us; we shall have need
To employ you towards this Roman. Come, our queen.

Exeunt all but CLOTEN

CLOTEN
If she be up, I'll speak with her; if not,
Let her lie still and dream.

Knocks

By your leave, ho!
I Know her women are about her: what
If I do line one of their hands? 'Tis gold
Which buys admittance; oft it doth; yea, and makes
Diana's rangers false themselves, yield up
Their deer to the stand o' the stealer; and 'tis gold
Which makes the true man kill'd and saves the thief;
Nay, sometime hangs both thief and true man: what
Can it not do and undo? I will make
One of her women lawyer to me, for
I yet not understand the case myself.

Knocks

By your leave.

Enter a LADY

LADY
Who's there that knocks?

CLOTEN

A gentleman.

LADY
No more?

CLOTEN
Yes, and a gentlewoman's son.

Lady
That's more
Than some, whose tailors are as dear as yours,
Can justly boast of. What's your lordship's pleasure?

CLOTEN
Your lady's person: is she ready?

LADY
Ay,
To keep her chamber.

CLOTEN
There is gold for you;
Sell me your good report.

LADY
How! my good name? or to report of you
What I shall think is good?—The princess!

Enter IMOGEN

CLOTEN
Good morrow, fairest: sister, your sweet hand.
Exit Lady

IMOGEN
Good morrow, sir. You lay out too much pains
For purchasing but trouble; the thanks I give
Is telling you that I am poor of thanks
And scarce can spare them.

CLOTEN
Still, I swear I love you.

IMOGEN
If you but said so, 'twere as deep with me:
If you swear still, your recompense is still
That I regard it not.

CLOTEN
This is no answer.

IMOGEN
But that you shall not say I yield being silent,
I would not speak. I pray you, spare me: 'faith,
I shall unfold equal discourtesy
To your best kindness: one of your great knowing
Should learn, being taught, forbearance.

CLOTEN
To leave you in your madness, 'twere my sin:
I will not.

IMOGEN
Fools are not mad folks.

CLOTEN
Do you call me fool?

IMOGEN
As I am mad, I do:
If you'll be patient, I'll no more be mad;
That cures us both. I am much sorry, sir,
You put me to forget a lady's manners,
By being so verbal: and learn now, for all,
That I, which know my heart, do here pronounce,
By the very truth of it, I care not for you,
And am so near the lack of charity—
To accuse myself—I hate you; which I had rather
You felt than make't my boast.

CLOTEN
You sin against
Obedience, which you owe your father. For
The contract you pretend with that base wretch,
One bred of alms and foster'd with cold dishes,
With scraps o' the court, it is no contract, none:
And though it be allow'd in meaner parties—
Yet who than he more mean?—to knit their souls,
On whom there is no more dependency
But brats and beggary, in self-figured knot;
Yet you are curb'd from that enlargement by
The consequence o' the crown, and must not soil
The precious note of it with a base slave.
A hilding for a livery, a squire's cloth,
A pantler, not so eminent.

IMOGEN
Profane fellow
Wert thou the son of Jupiter and no more
But what thou art besides, thou wert too base
To be his groom: thou wert dignified enough,
Even to the point of envy, if 'twere made

Comparative for your virtues, to be styled
The under-hangman of his kingdom, and hated
For being preferred so well.

CLOTEN
The south-fog rot him!

IMOGEN
He never can meet more mischance than come
To be but named of thee. His meanest garment,
That ever hath but clipp'd his body, is dearer
In my respect than all the hairs above thee,
Were they all made such men. How now, Pisanio!

Enter PISANIO

CLOTEN
'His garment!' Now the devil—

IMOGEN
To Dorothy my woman hie thee presently—

CLOTEN
'His garment!'

IMOGEN
I am sprited with a fool.
Frighted, and anger'd worse: go bid my woman
Search for a jewel that too casually
Hath left mine arm: it was thy master's: 'shrew me,
If I would lose it for a revenue
Of any king's in Europe. I do think
I saw't this morning: confident I am
Last night 'twas on mine arm; I kiss'd it:
I hope it be not gone to tell my lord
That I kiss aught but he.

PISANIO
'Twill not be lost.

IMOGEN
I hope so: go and search.

Exit PISANIO

CLOTEN
You have abused me:
'His meanest garment!'

IMOGEN

Ay, I said so, sir:
If you will make't an action, call witness to't.

CLOTEN
I will inform your father.

IMOGEN
Your mother too:
She's my good lady, and will conceive, I hope,
But the worst of me. So, I leave you, sir,
To the worst of discontent.

Exit

CLOTEN
I'll be revenged:
'His meanest garment!' Well.

Exit

SCENE IV. Rome. Philario's House.

Enter POSTHUMUS and PHILARIO

POSTHUMUS LEONATUS
Fear it not, sir: I would I were so sure
To win the king as I am bold her honour
Will remain hers.

PHILARIO
What means do you make to him?

POSTHUMUS LEONATUS
Not any, but abide the change of time,
Quake in the present winter's state and wish
That warmer days would come: in these sear'd hopes,
I barely gratify your love; they failing,
I must die much your debtor.

PHILARIO
Your very goodness and your company
O'erpays all I can do. By this, your king
Hath heard of great Augustus: Caius Lucius
Will do's commission throughly: and I think
He'll grant the tribute, send the arrearages,
Or look upon our Romans, whose remembrance
Is yet fresh in their grief.

POSTHUMUS LEONATUS

I do believe,
Statist though I am none, nor like to be,
That this will prove a war; and you shall hear
The legions now in Gallia sooner landed
In our not-fearing Britain than have tidings
Of any penny tribute paid. Our countrymen
Are men more order'd than when Julius Caesar
Smiled at their lack of skill, but found
their courage
Worthy his frowning at: their discipline,
Now mingled with their courages, will make known
To their approvers they are people such
That mend upon the world.

Enter IACHIMO

PHILARIO
See! Iachimo!

POSTHUMUS LEONATUS
The swiftest harts have posted you by land;
And winds of all the comers kiss'd your sails,
To make your vessel nimble.

PHILARIO
Welcome, sir.

POSTHUMUS LEONATUS
I hope the briefness of your answer made
The speediness of your return.

IACHIMO
Your lady
Is one of the fairest that I have look'd upon.

POSTHUMUS LEONATUS
And therewithal the best; or let her beauty
Look through a casement to allure false hearts
And be false with them.

IACHIMO
Here are letters for you.

POSTHUMUS LEONATUS
Their tenor good, I trust.

IACHIMO
'Tis very like.

PHILARIO

Was Caius Lucius in the Britain court
When you were there?

IACHIMO
He was expected then,
But not approach'd.

POSTHUMUS LEONATUS
All is well yet.
Sparkles this stone as it was wont? or is't not
Too dull for your good wearing?

IACHIMO
If I had lost it,
I should have lost the worth of it in gold.
I'll make a journey twice as far, to enjoy
A second night of such sweet shortness which
Was mine in Britain, for the ring is won.

POSTHUMUS LEONATUS
The stone's too hard to come by.

IACHIMO
Not a whit,
Your lady being so easy.

POSTHUMUS LEONATUS
Make not, sir,
Your loss your sport: I hope you know that we
Must not continue friends.

IACHIMO
Good sir, we must,
If you keep covenant. Had I not brought
The knowledge of your mistress home, I grant
We were to question further: but I now
Profess myself the winner of her honour,
Together with your ring; and not the wronger
Of her or you, having proceeded but
By both your wills.

POSTHUMUS LEONATUS
If you can make't apparent
That you have tasted her in bed, my hand
And ring is yours; if not, the foul opinion
You had of her pure honour gains or loses
Your sword or mine, or masterless leaves both
To who shall find them.

IACHIMO

Sir, my circumstances,
Being so near the truth as I will make them,
Must first induce you to believe: whose strength
I will confirm with oath; which, I doubt not,
You'll give me leave to spare, when you shall find
You need it not.

POSTHUMUS LEONATUS
Proceed.

IACHIMO
First, her bedchamber,—
Where, I confess, I slept not, but profess
Had that was well worth watching—it was hang'd
With tapesty of silk and silver; the story
Proud Cleopatra, when she met her Roman,
And Cydnus swell'd above the banks, or for
The press of boats or pride: a piece of work
So bravely done, so rich, that it did strive
In workmanship and value; which I wonder'd
Could be so rarely and exactly wrought,
Since the true life on't was—

POSTHUMUS LEONATUS
This is true;
And this you might have heard of here, by me,
Or by some other.

IACHIMO
More particulars
Must justify my knowledge.

POSTHUMUS LEONATUS
So they must,
Or do your honour injury.

IACHIMO
The chimney
Is south the chamber, and the chimney-piece
Chaste Dian bathing: never saw I figures
So likely to report themselves: the cutter
Was as another nature, dumb; outwent her,
Motion and breath left out.

POSTHUMUS LEONATUS
This is a thing
Which you might from relation likewise reap,
Being, as it is, much spoke of.

IACHIMO

The roof o' the chamber
With golden cherubins is fretted: her andirons—
I had forgot them—were two winking Cupids
Of silver, each on one foot standing, nicely
Depending on their brands.

POSTHUMUS LEONATUS
This is her honour!
Let it be granted you have seen all this—and praise
Be given to your remembrance—the description
Of what is in her chamber nothing saves
The wager you have laid.

IACHIMO
Then, if you can,

Showing the bracelet

Be pale: I beg but leave to air this jewel; see!
And now 'tis up again: it must be married
To that your diamond; I'll keep them.

POSTHUMUS LEONATUS
Jove!
Once more let me behold it: is it that
Which I left with her?

IACHIMO
Sir—I thank her—that:
She stripp'd it from her arm; I see her yet;
Her pretty action did outsell her gift,
And yet enrich'd it too: she gave it me, and said
She prized it once.

POSTHUMUS LEONATUS
May be she pluck'd it off
To send it me.

IACHIMO
She writes so to you, doth she?

POSTHUMUS LEONATUS
O, no, no, no! 'tis true. Here, take this too;

Gives the ring

It is a basilisk unto mine eye,
Kills me to look on't. Let there be no honour
Where there is beauty; truth, where semblance; love,
Where there's another man: the vows of women
Of no more bondage be, to where they are made,

Than they are to their virtues; which is nothing.
O, above measure false!

PHILARIO
Have patience, sir,
And take your ring again; 'tis not yet won:
It may be probable she lost it; or
Who knows if one of her women, being corrupted,
Hath stol'n it from her?

POSTHUMUS LEONATUS
Very true;
And so, I hope, he came by't. Back my ring:
Render to me some corporal sign about her,
More evident than this; for this was stolen.

IACHIMO
By Jupiter, I had it from her arm.

POSTHUMUS LEONATUS
Hark you, he swears; by Jupiter he swears.
'Tis true:—nay, keep the ring—'tis true: I am sure
She would not lose it: her attendants are
All sworn and honourable:—they induced to steal it!
And by a stranger!—No, he hath enjoyed her:
The cognizance of her incontinency
Is this: she hath bought the name of whore thus dearly.
There, take thy hire; and all the fiends of hell
Divide themselves between you!

PHILARIO
Sir, be patient:
This is not strong enough to be believed
Of one persuaded well of—

POSTHUMUS LEONATUS
Never talk on't;
She hath been colted by him.

IACHIMO
If you seek
For further satisfying, under her breast—
Worthy the pressing—lies a mole, right proud
Of that most delicate lodging: by my life,
I kiss'd it; and it gave me present hunger
To feed again, though full. You do remember
This stain upon her?

POSTHUMUS LEONATUS

Ay, and it doth confirm
Another stain, as big as hell can hold,
Were there no more but it.

IACHIMO
Will you hear more?

POSTHUMUS LEONATUS
Spare your arithmetic: never count the turns;
Once, and a million!

IACHIMO
I'll be sworn—

POSTHUMUS LEONATUS
No swearing.
If you will swear you have not done't, you lie;
And I will kill thee, if thou dost deny
Thou'st made me cuckold.

IACHIMO
I'll deny nothing.

POSTHUMUS LEONATUS
O, that I had her here, to tear her limb-meal!
I will go there and do't, i' the court, before
Her father. I'll do something—

Exit

PHILARIO
Quite besides
The government of patience! You have won:
Let's follow him, and pervert the present wrath
He hath against himself.

IACHIMO
With an my heart.

Exeunt

SCENE V. Another Room in Philario's House.

Enter POSTHUMUS LEONATUS

POSTHUMUS LEONATUS
Is there no way for men to be but women
Must be half-workers? We are all bastards;
And that most venerable man which I

Did call my father, was I know not where
When I was stamp'd; some coiner with his tools
Made me a counterfeit: yet my mother seem'd
The Dian of that time so doth my wife
The nonpareil of this. O, vengeance, vengeance!
Me of my lawful pleasure she restrain'd
And pray'd me oft forbearance; did it with
A pudency so rosy the sweet view on't
Might well have warm'd old Saturn; that I thought her
As chaste as unsunn'd snow. O, all the devils!
This yellow Iachimo, in an hour,—wast not?—
Or less,—at first?—perchance he spoke not, but,
Like a full-acorn'd boar, a German one,
Cried 'O!' and mounted; found no opposition
But what he look'd for should oppose and she
Should from encounter guard. Could I find out
The woman's part in me! For there's no motion
That tends to vice in man, but I affirm
It is the woman's part: be it lying, note it,
The woman's; flattering, hers; deceiving, hers;
Lust and rank thoughts, hers, hers; revenges, hers;
Ambitions, covetings, change of prides, disdain,
Nice longing, slanders, mutability,
All faults that may be named, nay, that hell knows,
Why, hers, in part or all; but rather, all;
For even to vice
They are not constant but are changing still
One vice, but of a minute old, for one
Not half so old as that. I'll write against them,
Detest them, curse them: yet 'tis greater skill
In a true hate, to pray they have their will:
The very devils cannot plague them better.

Exit

ACT III

SCENE I. Britain. A Hall in Cymbeline's Palace.

Enter in state, CYMBELINE, QUEEN, CLOTEN, and LORDS at one door, and at another, CAIUS LUCIUS and ATTENDANTS

CYMBELINE
Now say, what would Augustus Caesar with us?

CAIUS LUCIUS
When Julius Caesar, whose remembrance yet
Lives in men's eyes and will to ears and tongues

Be theme and hearing ever, was in this Britain
And conquer'd it, Cassibelan, thine uncle,—
Famous in Caesar's praises, no whit less
Than in his feats deserving it—for him
And his succession granted Rome a tribute,
Yearly three thousand pounds, which by thee lately
Is left untender'd.

QUEEN
And, to kill the marvel,
Shall be so ever.

CLOTEN
There be many Caesars,
Ere such another Julius. Britain is
A world by itself; and we will nothing pay
For wearing our own noses.

QUEEN
That opportunity
Which then they had to take from 's, to resume
We have again. Remember, sir, my liege,
The kings your ancestors, together with
The natural bravery of your isle, which stands
As Neptune's park, ribbed and paled in
With rocks unscalable and roaring waters,
With sands that will not bear your enemies' boats,
But suck them up to the topmast. A kind of conquest
Caesar made here; but made not here his brag
Of 'Came' and 'saw' and 'overcame: ' with shame—
That first that ever touch'd him—he was carried
From off our coast, twice beaten; and his shipping—
Poor ignorant baubles!— upon our terrible seas,
Like egg-shells moved upon their surges, crack'd
As easily 'gainst our rocks: for joy whereof
The famed Cassibelan, who was once at point—
O giglot fortune!—to master Caesar's sword,
Made Lud's town with rejoicing fires bright
And Britons strut with courage.

CLOTEN
Come, there's no more tribute to be paid: our
kingdom is stronger than it was at that time; and,
as I said, there is no moe such Caesars: other of
them may have crook'd noses, but to owe such
straight arms, none.

CYMBELINE
Son, let your mother end.

CLOTEN

We have yet many among us can gripe as hard as
Cassibelan: I do not say I am one; but I have a
hand. Why tribute? why should we pay tribute? If
Caesar can hide the sun from us with a blanket, or
put the moon in his pocket, we will pay him tribute
for light; else, sir, no more tribute, pray you now.

CYMBELINE
You must know,
Till the injurious Romans did extort
This tribute from us, we were free:
Caesar's ambition,
Which swell'd so much that it did almost stretch
The sides o' the world, against all colour here
Did put the yoke upon 's; which to shake off
Becomes a warlike people, whom we reckon
Ourselves to be.

CLOTEN Lords
We do.

CYMBELINE
Say, then, to Caesar,
Our ancestor was that Mulmutius which
Ordain'd our laws, whose use the sword of Caesar
Hath too much mangled; whose repair and franchise
Shall, by the power we hold, be our good deed,
Though Rome be therefore angry: Mulmutius made our laws,
Who was the first of Britain which did put
His brows within a golden crown and call'd
Himself a king.

CAIUS LUCIUS
I am sorry, Cymbeline,
That I am to pronounce Augustus Caesar—
Caesar, that hath more kings his servants than
Thyself domestic officers—thine enemy:
Receive it from me, then: war and confusion
In Caesar's name pronounce I 'gainst thee: look
For fury not to be resisted. Thus defied,
I thank thee for myself.

CYMBELINE
Thou art welcome, Caius.
Thy Caesar knighted me; my youth I spent
Much under him; of him I gather'd honour;
Which he to seek of me again, perforce,
Behoves me keep at utterance. I am perfect
That the Pannonians and Dalmatians for
Their liberties are now in arms; a precedent

Which not to read would show the Britons cold:
So Caesar shall not find them.

CAIUS LUCIUS
Let proof speak.

CLOTEN
His majesty bids you welcome. Make
pastime with us a day or two, or longer: if
you seek us afterwards in other terms, you
shall find us in our salt-water girdle: if you
beat us out of it, it is yours; if you fall in
the adventure, our crows shall fare the better
for you; and there's an end.

CAIUS LUCIUS
So, sir.

CYMBELINE
I know your master's pleasure and he mine:
All the remain is 'Welcome!'

Exeunt

SCENE II. Another Room in the Palace.

Enter PISANIO, with a letter

PISANIO
How? of adultery? Wherefore write you not
What monster's her accuser? Leonatus,
O master! what a strange infection
Is fall'n into thy ear! What false Italian,
As poisonous-tongued as handed, hath prevail'd
On thy too ready hearing? Disloyal! No:
She's punish'd for her truth, and undergoes,
More goddess-like than wife-like, such assaults
As would take in some virtue. O my master!
Thy mind to her is now as low as were
Thy fortunes. How! that I should murder her?
Upon the love and truth and vows which I
Have made to thy command? I, her? her blood?
If it be so to do good service, never
Let me be counted serviceable. How look I,
That I should seem to lack humanity
so much as this fact comes to?

Reading

'Do't: the letter
that I have sent her, by her own command
Shall give thee opportunity.' O damn'd paper!
Black as the ink that's on thee! Senseless bauble,
Art thou a feodary for this act, and look'st
So virgin-like without? Lo, here she comes.
I am ignorant in what I am commanded.

Enter IMOGEN

IMOGEN
How now, Pisanio!

PISANIO
Madam, here is a letter from my lord.

IMOGEN
Who? thy lord? that is my lord, Leonatus!
O, learn'd indeed were that astronomer
That knew the stars as I his characters;
He'ld lay the future open. You good gods,
Let what is here contain'd relish of love,
Of my lord's health, of his content, yet not
That we two are asunder; let that grieve him:
Some griefs are med'cinable; that is one of them,
For it doth physic love: of his content,
All but in that! Good wax, thy leave. Blest be
You bees that make these locks of counsel! Lovers
And men in dangerous bonds pray not alike:
Though forfeiters you cast in prison, yet
You clasp young Cupid's tables. Good news, gods!

Reads

'Justice, and your father's wrath, should he take me in his dominion, could not be so cruel to me, as you, O the dearest of creatures, would even renew me with your eyes. Take notice that I am in Cambria, at Milford-Haven: what your own love will out of this advise you, follow. So he wishes you all happiness, that remains loyal to his vow, and your, increasing in love, LEONATUS POSTHUMUS.'

O, for a horse with wings! Hear'st thou, Pisanio?
He is at Milford-Haven: read, and tell me
How far 'tis thither. If one of mean affairs
May plod it in a week, why may not I
Glide thither in a day? Then, true Pisanio,—
Who long'st, like me, to see thy lord; who long'st,—
let me bate,-but not like me—yet long'st,
But in a fainter kind:—O, not like me;
For mine's beyond beyond—say, and speak thick;
Love's counsellor should fill the bores of hearing,
To the smothering of the sense—how far it is
To this same blessed Milford: and by the way

Tell me how Wales was made so happy as
To inherit such a haven: but first of all,
How we may steal from hence, and for the gap
That we shall make in time, from our hence-going
And our return, to excuse: but first, how get hence:
Why should excuse be born or e'er begot?
We'll talk of that hereafter. Prithee, speak,
How many score of miles may we well ride
'Twixt hour and hour?

PISANIO
One score 'twixt sun and sun,
Madam, 's enough for you:

Aside
and too much too.

IMOGEN
Why, one that rode to's execution, man,
Could never go so slow: I have heard of riding wagers,
Where horses have been nimbler than the sands
That run i' the clock's behalf. But this is foolery:
Go bid my woman feign a sickness; say
She'll home to her father: and provide me presently
A riding-suit, no costlier than would fit
A franklin's housewife.

PISANIO
Madam, you're best consider.

IMOGEN
I see before me, man: nor here, nor here,
Nor what ensues, but have a fog in them,
That I cannot look through. Away, I prithee;
Do as I bid thee: there's no more to say,
Accessible is none but Milford way.

Exeunt

SCENE III. Wales: a Mountainous Country with a Cave.

Enter, from the cave, BELARIUS; GUIDERIUS, and ARVIRAGUS following

BELARIUS
A goodly day not to keep house, with such
Whose roof's as low as ours! Stoop, boys; this gate
Instructs you how to adore the heavens and bows you
To a morning's holy office: the gates of monarchs
Are arch'd so high that giants may jet through

And keep their impious turbans on, without
Good morrow to the sun. Hail, thou fair heaven!
We house i' the rock, yet use thee not so hardly
As prouder livers do.

GUIDERIUS
Hail, heaven!

ARVIRAGUS
Hail, heaven!

BELARIUS
Now for our mountain sport: up to yond hill;
Your legs are young; I'll tread these flats. Consider,
When you above perceive me like a crow,
That it is place which lessens and sets off;
And you may then revolve what tales I have told you
Of courts, of princes, of the tricks in war:
This service is not service, so being done,
But being so allow'd: to apprehend thus,
Draws us a profit from all things we see;
And often, to our comfort, shall we find
The sharded beetle in a safer hold
Than is the full-wing'd eagle. O, this life
Is nobler than attending for a cheque,
Richer than doing nothing for a bauble,
Prouder than rustling in unpaid-for silk:
Such gain the cap of him that makes 'em fine,
Yet keeps his book uncross'd: no life to ours.

GUIDERIUS
Out of your proof you speak: we, poor unfledged,
Have never wing'd from view o' the nest, nor know not
What air's from home. Haply this life is best,
If quiet life be best; sweeter to you
That have a sharper known; well corresponding
With your stiff age: but unto us it is
A cell of ignorance; travelling a-bed;
A prison for a debtor, that not dares
To stride a limit.

ARVIRAGUS
What should we speak of
When we are old as you? when we shall hear
The rain and wind beat dark December, how,
In this our pinching cave, shall we discourse
The freezing hours away? We have seen nothing;
We are beastly, subtle as the fox for prey,
Like warlike as the wolf for what we eat;
Our valour is to chase what flies; our cage

We make a quire, as doth the prison'd bird,
And sing our bondage freely.

BELARIUS
How you speak!
Did you but know the city's usuries
And felt them knowingly; the art o' the court
As hard to leave as keep; whose top to climb
Is certain falling, or so slippery that
The fear's as bad as falling; the toil o' the war,
A pain that only seems to seek out danger
I' the name of fame and honour; which dies i' the search,
And hath as oft a slanderous epitaph
As record of fair act; nay, many times,
Doth ill deserve by doing well; what's worse,
Must court'sy at the censure:—O boys, this story
The world may read in me: my body's mark'd
With Roman swords, and my report was once
First with the best of note: Cymbeline loved me,
And when a soldier was the theme, my name
Was not far off: then was I as a tree
Whose boughs did bend with fruit: but in one night,
A storm or robbery, call it what you will,
Shook down my mellow hangings, nay, my leaves,
And left me bare to weather.

GUIDERIUS
Uncertain favour!

BELARIUS
My fault being nothing—as I have told you oft—
But that two villains, whose false oaths prevail'd
Before my perfect honour, swore to Cymbeline
I was confederate with the Romans: so
Follow'd my banishment, and this twenty years
This rock and these demesnes have been my world;
Where I have lived at honest freedom, paid
More pious debts to heaven than in all
The fore-end of my time. But up to the mountains!
This is not hunters' language: he that strikes
The venison first shall be the lord o' the feast;
To him the other two shall minister;
And we will fear no poison, which attends
In place of greater state. I'll meet you in the valleys.

Exeunt GUIDERIUS and ARVIRAGUS

How hard it is to hide the sparks of nature!
These boys know little they are sons to the king;
Nor Cymbeline dreams that they are alive.
They think they are mine; and though train'd up thus meanly

I' the cave wherein they bow, their thoughts do hit
The roofs of palaces, and nature prompts them
In simple and low things to prince it much
Beyond the trick of others. This Polydore,
The heir of Cymbeline and Britain, who
The king his father call'd Guiderius,—Jove!
When on my three-foot stool I sit and tell
The warlike feats I have done, his spirits fly out
Into my story: say 'Thus, mine enemy fell,
And thus I set my foot on 's neck;' even then
The princely blood flows in his cheek, he sweats,
Strains his young nerves and puts himself in posture
That acts my words. The younger brother, Cadwal,
Once Arviragus, in as like a figure,
Strikes life into my speech and shows much more
His own conceiving.—Hark, the game is roused!
O Cymbeline! heaven and my conscience knows
Thou didst unjustly banish me: whereon,
At three and two years old, I stole these babes;
Thinking to bar thee of succession, as
Thou reft'st me of my lands. Euriphile,
Thou wast their nurse; they took thee for their mother,
And every day do honour to her grave:
Myself, Belarius, that am Morgan call'd,
They take for natural father. The game is up.

Exit

SCENE IV. Country Near Milford-Haven.

Enter PISANIO and IMOGEN

IMOGEN
Thou told'st me, when we came from horse, the place
Was near at hand: ne'er long'd my mother so
To see me first, as I have now. Pisanio! man!
Where is Posthumus? What is in thy mind,
That makes thee stare thus? Wherefore breaks that sigh
From the inward of thee? One, but painted thus,
Would be interpreted a thing perplex'd
Beyond self-explication: put thyself
Into a havior of less fear, ere wildness
Vanquish my staider senses. What's the matter?
Why tender'st thou that paper to me, with
A look untender? If't be summer news,
Smile to't before; if winterly, thou need'st
But keep that countenance still. My husband's hand!
That drug-damn'd Italy hath out-craftied him,
And he's at some hard point. Speak, man: thy tongue

May take off some extremity, which to read
Would be even mortal to me.

PISANIO
Please you, read;
And you shall find me, wretched man, a thing
The most disdain'd of fortune.

IMOGEN
[Reads] 'Thy mistress, Pisanio, hath played the strumpet in my bed; the testimonies whereof lie bleeding in me. I speak not out of weak surmises, but from proof as strong as my grief and as certain as I expect my revenge. That part thou, Pisanio, must act for me, if thy faith be not tainted with the breach of hers. Let thine own hands take away her life: I shall give thee opportunity at Milford-Haven. She hath my letter for the purpose where, if thou fear to strike and to make me certain it is done, thou art the pandar to her dishonour and equally to me disloyal.'

PISANIO
What shall I need to draw my sword? the paper
Hath cut her throat already. No, 'tis slander,
Whose edge is sharper than the sword, whose tongue
Outvenoms all the worms of Nile, whose breath
Rides on the posting winds and doth belie
All corners of the world: kings, queens and states,
Maids, matrons, nay, the secrets of the grave
This viperous slander enters. What cheer, madam?

IMOGEN
False to his bed! What is it to be false?
To lie in watch there and to think on him?
To weep 'twixt clock and clock? if sleep charge nature,
To break it with a fearful dream of him
And cry myself awake? that's false to's bed, is it?

PISANIO
Alas, good lady!

IMOGEN
I false! Thy conscience witness: Iachimo,
Thou didst accuse him of incontinency;
Thou then look'dst like a villain; now methinks
Thy favour's good enough. Some jay of Italy
Whose mother was her painting, hath betray'd him:
Poor I am stale, a garment out of fashion;
And, for I am richer than to hang by the walls,
I must be ripp'd:—to pieces with me!—O,
Men's vows are women's traitors! All good seeming,
By thy revolt, O husband, shall be thought
Put on for villany; not born where't grows,
But worn a bait for ladies.

PISANIO

Good madam, hear me.

IMOGEN
True honest men being heard, like false Aeneas,
Were in his time thought false, and Sinon's weeping
Did scandal many a holy tear, took pity
From most true wretchedness: so thou, Posthumus,
Wilt lay the leaven on all proper men;
Goodly and gallant shall be false and perjured
From thy great fall. Come, fellow, be thou honest:
Do thou thy master's bidding: when thou see'st him,
A little witness my obedience: look!
I draw the sword myself: take it, and hit
The innocent mansion of my love, my heart;
Fear not; 'tis empty of all things but grief;
Thy master is not there, who was indeed
The riches of it: do his bidding; strike
Thou mayst be valiant in a better cause;
But now thou seem'st a coward.

PISANIO
Hence, vile instrument!
Thou shalt not damn my hand.

IMOGEN
Why, I must die;
And if I do not by thy hand, thou art
No servant of thy master's. Against self-slaughter
There is a prohibition so divine
That cravens my weak hand. Come, here's my heart.
Something's afore't. Soft, soft! we'll no defence;
Obedient as the scabbard. What is here?
The scriptures of the loyal Leonatus,
All turn'd to heresy? Away, away,
Corrupters of my faith! you shall no more
Be stomachers to my heart. Thus may poor fools
Believe false teachers: though those that are betray'd
Do feel the treason sharply, yet the traitor
Stands in worse case of woe.
And thou, Posthumus, thou that didst set up
My disobedience 'gainst the king my father
And make me put into contempt the suits
Of princely fellows, shalt hereafter find
It is no act of common passage, but
A strain of rareness: and I grieve myself
To think, when thou shalt be disedged by her
That now thou tirest on, how thy memory
Will then be pang'd by me. Prithee, dispatch:
The lamb entreats the butcher: where's thy knife?
Thou art too slow to do thy master's bidding,
When I desire it too.

PISANIO
O gracious lady,
Since I received command to do this business
I have not slept one wink.

IMOGEN
Do't, and to bed then.

PISANIO
I'll wake mine eye-balls blind first.

IMOGEN
Wherefore then
Didst undertake it? Why hast thou abused
So many miles with a pretence? this place?
Mine action and thine own? our horses' labour?
The time inviting thee? the perturb'd court,
For my being absent? whereunto I never
Purpose return. Why hast thou gone so far,
To be unbent when thou hast ta'en thy stand,
The elected deer before thee?

PISANIO
But to win time
To lose so bad employment; in the which
I have consider'd of a course. Good lady,
Hear me with patience.

IMOGEN
Talk thy tongue weary; speak
I have heard I am a strumpet; and mine ear
Therein false struck, can take no greater wound,
Nor tent to bottom that. But speak.

PISANIO
Then, madam,
I thought you would not back again.

IMOGEN
Most like;
Bringing me here to kill me.

PISANIO
Not so, neither:
But if I were as wise as honest, then
My purpose would prove well. It cannot be
But that my master is abused:
Some villain, ay, and singular in his art.
Hath done you both this cursed injury.

IMOGEN
Some Roman courtezan.

PISANIO
No, on my life.
I'll give but notice you are dead and send him
Some bloody sign of it; for 'tis commanded
I should do so: you shall be miss'd at court,
And that will well confirm it.

IMOGEN
Why good fellow,
What shall I do the where? where bide? how live?
Or in my life what comfort, when I am
Dead to my husband?

PISANIO
If you'll back to the court—

IMOGEN
No court, no father; nor no more ado
With that harsh, noble, simple nothing,
That Cloten, whose love-suit hath been to me
As fearful as a siege.

PISANIO
If not at court,
Then not in Britain must you bide.

IMOGEN
Where then
Hath Britain all the sun that shines? Day, night,
Are they not but in Britain? I' the world's volume
Our Britain seems as of it, but not in 't;
In a great pool a swan's nest: prithee, think
There's livers out of Britain.

PISANIO
I am most glad
You think of other place. The ambassador,
Lucius the Roman, comes to Milford-Haven
To-morrow: now, if you could wear a mind
Dark as your fortune is, and but disguise
That which, to appear itself, must not yet be
But by self-danger, you should tread a course
Pretty and full of view; yea, haply, near
The residence of Posthumus; so nigh at least
That though his actions were not visible, yet
Report should render him hourly to your ear
As truly as he moves.

IMOGEN
O, for such means!
Though peril to my modesty, not death on't,
I would adventure.

PISANIO
Well, then, here's the point:
You must forget to be a woman; change
Command into obedience: fear and niceness—
The handmaids of all women, or, more truly,
Woman its pretty self—into a waggish courage:
Ready in gibes, quick-answer'd, saucy and
As quarrelous as the weasel; nay, you must
Forget that rarest treasure of your cheek,
Exposing it—but, O, the harder heart!
Alack, no remedy!—to the greedy touch
Of common-kissing Titan, and forget
Your laboursome and dainty trims, wherein
You made great Juno angry.

IMOGEN
Nay, be brief
I see into thy end, and am almost
A man already.

PISANIO
First, make yourself but like one.
Fore-thinking this, I have already fit—
'Tis in my cloak-bag—doublet, hat, hose, all
That answer to them: would you in their serving,
And with what imitation you can borrow
From youth of such a season, 'fore noble Lucius
Present yourself, desire his service, tell him
wherein you're happy,—which you'll make him know,
If that his head have ear in music,—doubtless
With joy he will embrace you, for he's honourable
And doubling that, most holy. Your means abroad,
You have me, rich; and I will never fail
Beginning nor supplyment.

IMOGEN
Thou art all the comfort
The gods will diet me with. Prithee, away:
There's more to be consider'd; but we'll even
All that good time will give us: this attempt
I am soldier to, and will abide it with
A prince's courage. Away, I prithee.

PISANIO
Well, madam, we must take a short farewell,
Lest, being miss'd, I be suspected of

Your carriage from the court. My noble mistress,
Here is a box; I had it from the queen:
What's in't is precious; if you are sick at sea,
Or stomach-qualm'd at land, a dram of this
Will drive away distemper. To some shade,
And fit you to your manhood. May the gods
Direct you to the best!

IMOGEN
Amen: I thank thee.

Exeunt, severally

SCENE V. A Room in Cymbeline's Palace.

Enter CYMBELINE, QUEEN, CLOTEN, LUCIUS, LORDS, and ATTENDANTS

CYMBELINE
Thus far; and so farewell.

CAIUS LUCIUS
Thanks, royal sir.
My emperor hath wrote, I must from hence;
And am right sorry that I must report ye
My master's enemy.

CYMBELINE
Our subjects, sir,
Will not endure his yoke; and for ourself
To show less sovereignty than they, must needs
Appear unkinglike.

CAIUS LUCIUS
So, sir: I desire of you
A conduct over-land to Milford-Haven.
Madam, all joy befal your grace!

QUEEN
And you!

CYMBELINE
My lords, you are appointed for that office;
The due of honour in no point omit.
So farewell, noble Lucius.

CAIUS LUCIUS
Your hand, my lord.

CLOTEN

Receive it friendly; but from this time forth
I wear it as your enemy.

CAIUS LUCIUS
Sir, the event
Is yet to name the winner: fare you well.

CYMBELINE
Leave not the worthy Lucius, good my lords,
Till he have cross'd the Severn. Happiness!

Exeunt LUCIUS and LORDS

QUEEN
He goes hence frowning: but it honours us
That we have given him cause.

CLOTEN
'Tis all the better;
Your valiant Britons have their wishes in it.

CYMBELINE
Lucius hath wrote already to the emperor
How it goes here. It fits us therefore ripely
Our chariots and our horsemen be in readiness:
The powers that he already hath in Gallia
Will soon be drawn to head, from whence he moves
His war for Britain.

QUEEN
'Tis not sleepy business;
But must be look'd to speedily and strongly.

CYMBELINE
Our expectation that it would be thus
Hath made us forward. But, my gentle queen,
Where is our daughter? She hath not appear'd
Before the Roman, nor to us hath tender'd
The duty of the day: she looks us like
A thing more made of malice than of duty:
We have noted it. Call her before us; for
We have been too slight in sufferance.

Exit an ATTENDANT

QUEEN
Royal sir,
Since the exile of Posthumus, most retired
Hath her life been; the cure whereof, my lord,
'Tis time must do. Beseech your majesty,
Forbear sharp speeches to her: she's a lady

So tender of rebukes that words are strokes
And strokes death to her.

Re-enter ATTENDANT

CYMBELINE
Where is she, sir? How
Can her contempt be answer'd?

ATTENDANT
Please you, sir,
Her chambers are all lock'd; and there's no answer
That will be given to the loudest noise we make.

QUEEN
My lord, when last I went to visit her,
She pray'd me to excuse her keeping close,
Whereto constrain'd by her infirmity,
She should that duty leave unpaid to you,
Which daily she was bound to proffer: this
She wish'd me to make known; but our great court
Made me to blame in memory.

CYMBELINE
Her doors lock'd?
Not seen of late? Grant, heavens, that which I fear
Prove false!

Exit

QUEEN
Son, I say, follow the king.

CLOTEN
That man of hers, Pisanio, her old servant,
have not seen these two days.

QUEEN
Go, look after.

Exit CLOTEN

Pisanio, thou that stand'st so for Posthumus!
He hath a drug of mine; I pray his absence
Proceed by swallowing that, for he believes
It is a thing most precious. But for her,
Where is she gone? Haply, despair hath seized her,
Or, wing'd with fervor of her love, she's flown
To her desired Posthumus: gone she is
To death or to dishonour; and my end

Can make good use of either: she being down,
I have the placing of the British crown.

Re-enter CLOTEN

How now, my son!

CLOTEN
'Tis certain she is fled.
Go in and cheer the king: he rages; none
Dare come about him.

QUEEN
[Aside] All the better: may
This night forestall him of the coming day!

Exit

CLOTEN
I love and hate her: for she's fair and royal,
And that she hath all courtly parts more exquisite
Than lady, ladies, woman; from every one
The best she hath, and she, of all compounded,
Outsells them all; I love her therefore: but
Disdaining me and throwing favours on
The low Posthumus slanders so her judgment
That what's else rare is choked; and in that point
I will conclude to hate her, nay, indeed,
To be revenged upon her. For when fools Shall—

Enter PISANIO

Who is here? What, are you packing, sirrah?
Come hither: ah, you precious pander! Villain,
Where is thy lady? In a word; or else
Thou art straightway with the fiends.

PISANIO
O, good my lord!

CLOTEN
Where is thy lady? Or, by Jupiter,—
I will not ask again. Close villain,
I'll have this secret from thy heart, or rip
Thy heart to find it. Is she with Posthumus?
From whose so many weights of baseness cannot
A dram of worth be drawn.

PISANIO

Alas, my lord,
How can she be with him? When was she missed?
He is in Rome.

CLOTEN
Where is she, sir? Come nearer;
No further halting: satisfy me home
What is become of her.

PISANIO
O, my all-worthy lord!

CLOTEN
All-worthy villain!
Discover where thy mistress is at once,
At the next word: no more of 'worthy lord!'
Speak, or thy silence on the instant is
Thy condemnation and thy death.

PISANIO
Then, sir,
This paper is the history of my knowledge
Touching her flight.

Presenting a letter

CLOTEN
Let's see't. I will pursue her
Even to Augustus' throne.

PISANIO
[Aside] Or this, or perish.
She's far enough; and what he learns by this
May prove his travel, not her danger.

CLOTEN
Hum!

PISANIO
[Aside] I'll write to my lord she's dead. O Imogen,
Safe mayst thou wander, safe return again!

CLOTEN
Sirrah, is this letter true?

PISANIO
Sir, as I think.

CLOTEN
It is Posthumus' hand; I know't. Sirrah, if thou wouldst not be a villain, but do me true service, undergo those employments wherein I should have cause to use thee with a serious industry, that is,

what villany soe'er I bid thee do, to perform it directly and truly, I would think thee an honest man: thou shouldst neither want my means for thy relief nor my voice for thy preferment.

PISANIO
Well, my good lord.

CLOTEN
Wilt thou serve me? for since patiently and constantly thou hast stuck to the bare fortune of that beggar Posthumus, thou canst not, in the course of gratitude, but be a diligent follower of mine: wilt thou serve me?

PISANIO
Sir, I will.

CLOTEN
Give me thy hand; here's my purse. Hast any of thy late master's garments in thy possession?

PISANIO
I have, my lord, at my lodging, the same suit he wore when he took leave of my lady and mistress.

CLOTEN
The first service thou dost me, fetch that suit hither: let it be thy lint service; go.

PISANIO
I shall, my lord.

Exit

CLOTEN
Meet thee at Milford-Haven!—I forgot to ask him one thing; I'll remember't anon:—even there, thou villain Posthumus, will I kill thee. I would these garments were come. She said upon a time—the bitterness of it I now belch from my heart—that she held the very garment of Posthumus in more respect than my noble and natural person together with the adornment of my qualities. With that suit upon my back, will I ravish her: first kill him, and in her eyes; there shall she see my valour, which will then be a torment to her contempt. He on the ground, my speech of insultment ended on his dead body, and when my lust hath dined,—which, as I say, to vex her I will execute in the clothes that she so praised,—to the court I'll knock her back, foot her home again. She hath despised me rejoicingly, and I'll be merry in my revenge.

Re-enter PISANIO, with the clothes

Be those the garments?

PISANIO
Ay, my noble lord.

CLOTEN
How long is't since she went to Milford-Haven?

PISANIO
She can scarce be there yet.

CLOTEN

Bring this apparel to my chamber; that is the second thing that I have commanded thee: the third is, that thou wilt be a voluntary mute to my design. Be but duteous, and true preferment shall tender itself to thee. My revenge is now at Milford: would I had wings to follow it! Come, and be true.

Exit

PISANIO

Thou bid'st me to my loss: for true to thee
Were to prove false, which I will never be,
To him that is most true. To Milford go,
And find not her whom thou pursuest. Flow, flow,
You heavenly blessings, on her! This fool's speed
Be cross'd with slowness; labour be his meed!

Exit

SCENE VI. Wales. Before the Cave of Belarius.

Enter IMOGEN, in boy's clothes

IMOGEN

I see a man's life is a tedious one:
I have tired myself, and for two nights together
Have made the ground my bed. I should be sick,
But that my resolution helps me. Milford,
When from the mountain-top Pisanio show'd thee,
Thou wast within a ken: O Jove! I think
Foundations fly the wretched; such, I mean,
Where they should be relieved. Two beggars told me
I could not miss my way: will poor folks lie,
That have afflictions on them, knowing 'tis
A punishment or trial? Yes; no wonder,
When rich ones scarce tell true. To lapse in fulness
Is sorer than to lie for need, and falsehood
Is worse in kings than beggars. My dear lord!
Thou art one o' the false ones. Now I think on thee,
My hunger's gone; but even before, I was
At point to sink for food. But what is this?
Here is a path to't: 'tis some savage hold:
I were best not to call; I dare not call: yet famine,
Ere clean it o'erthrow nature, makes it valiant,
Plenty and peace breeds cowards: hardness ever
Of hardiness is mother. Ho! who's here?
If any thing that's civil, speak; if savage,
Take or lend. Ho! No answer? Then I'll enter.
Best draw my sword: and if mine enemy

But fear the sword like me, he'll scarcely look on't.
Such a foe, good heavens!

Exit, to the cave

Enter BELARIUS, GUIDERIUS, and ARVIRAGUS

BELARIUS
You, Polydote, have proved best woodman and
Are master of the feast: Cadwal and I
Will play the cook and servant; 'tis our match:
The sweat of industry would dry and die,
But for the end it works to. Come; our stomachs
Will make what's homely savoury: weariness
Can snore upon the flint, when resty sloth
Finds the down pillow hard. Now peace be here,
Poor house, that keep'st thyself!

GUIDERIUS
I am thoroughly weary.

ARVIRAGUS
I am weak with toil, yet strong in appetite.

GUIDERIUS
There is cold meat i' the cave; we'll browse on that,
Whilst what we have kill'd be cook'd.

BELARIUS
[Looking into the cave]
Stay; come not in.
But that it eats our victuals, I should think
Here were a fairy.

GUIDERIUS
What's the matter, sir?

BELARIUS
By Jupiter, an angel! or, if not,
An earthly paragon! Behold divineness
No elder than a boy!

Re-enter IMOGEN

IMOGEN
Good masters, harm me not:
Before I enter'd here, I call'd; and thought
To have begg'd or bought what I have took: good troth,
I have stol'n nought, nor would not, though I had found
Gold strew'd i' the floor. Here's money for my meat:
I would have left it on the board so soon

As I had made my meal, and parted
With prayers for the provider.

GUIDERIUS
Money, youth?

ARVIRAGUS
All gold and silver rather turn to dirt!
As 'tis no better reckon'd, but of those
Who worship dirty gods.

IMOGEN
I see you're angry:
Know, if you kill me for my fault, I should
Have died had I not made it.

BELARIUS
Whither bound?

IMOGEN
To Milford-Haven.

BELARIUS
What's your name?

IMOGEN
Fidele, sir. I have a kinsman who
Is bound for Italy; he embark'd at Milford;
To whom being going, almost spent with hunger,
I am fall'n in this offence.

BELARIUS
Prithee, fair youth,
Think us no churls, nor measure our good minds
By this rude place we live in. Well encounter'd!
'Tis almost night: you shall have better cheer
Ere you depart: and thanks to stay and eat it.
Boys, bid him welcome.

GUIDERIUS
Were you a woman, youth,
I should woo hard but be your groom. In honesty,
I bid for you as I'd buy.

ARVIRAGUS
I'll make't my comfort
He is a man; I'll love him as my brother:
And such a welcome as I'd give to him
After long absence, such is yours: most welcome!
Be sprightly, for you fall 'mongst friends.

IMOGEN
'Mongst friends,
If brothers.

Aside

Would it had been so, that they
Had been my father's sons! then had my prize
Been less, and so more equal ballasting
To thee, Posthumus.

BELARIUS
He wrings at some distress.

GUIDERIUS
Would I could free't!

ARVIRAGUS
Or I, whate'er it be,
What pain it cost, what danger. God's!

BELARIUS
Hark, boys.

Whispering

IMOGEN
Great men,
That had a court no bigger than this cave,
That did attend themselves and had the virtue
Which their own conscience seal'd them—laying by
That nothing-gift of differing multitudes—
Could not out-peer these twain. Pardon me, gods!
I'd change my sex to be companion with them,
Since Leonatus's false.

BELARIUS
It shall be so.
Boys, we'll go dress our hunt. Fair youth, come in:
Discourse is heavy, fasting; when we have supp'd,
We'll mannerly demand thee of thy story,
So far as thou wilt speak it.

GUIDERIUS
Pray, draw near.

ARVIRAGUS
The night to the owl and morn to the lark
less welcome.

IMOGEN

Thanks, sir.

ARVIRAGUS
I pray, draw near.

Exeunt

SCENE VII. Rome. A Public Place.

Enter two SENATORS and TRIBUNES

FIRST SENATOR
This is the tenor of the emperor's writ:
That since the common men are now in action
'Gainst the Pannonians and Dalmatians,
And that the legions now in Gallia are
Full weak to undertake our wars against
The fall'n-off Britons, that we do incite
The gentry to this business. He creates
Lucius preconsul: and to you the tribunes,
For this immediate levy, he commends
His absolute commission. Long live Caesar!

FIRST TRIBUNE
Is Lucius general of the forces?

SECOND SENATOR
Ay.

FIRST TRIBUNE
Remaining now in Gallia?

FIRST SENATOR
With those legions
Which I have spoke of, whereunto your levy
Must be supplyant: the words of your commission
Will tie you to the numbers and the time
Of their dispatch.

FIRST TRIBUNE
We will discharge our duty.

Exeunt

ACT IV

SCENE I. Wales: Near the Cave of Belarius.

Enter CLOTEN

CLOTEN
I am near to the place where they should meet, if Pisanio have mapped it truly. How fit his garments serve me! Why should his mistress, who was made by him that made the tailor, not be fit too? the rather—saving reverence of the word—for 'tis said a woman's fitness comes by fits. Therein I must play the workman. I dare speak it to myself—for it is not vain-glory for a man and his glass to confer in his own chamber—I mean, the lines of my body are as well drawn as his; no less young, more strong, not beneath him in fortunes, beyond him in the advantage of the time, above him in birth, alike conversant in general services, and more remarkable in single oppositions: yet this imperceiverant thing loves him in my despite. What mortality is! Posthumus, thy head, which now is growing upon thy shoulders, shall within this hour be off; thy mistress enforced; thy garments cut to pieces before thy face: and all this done, spurn her home to her father; who may haply be a little angry for my so rough usage; but my mother, having power of his testiness, shall turn all into my commendations. My horse is tied up safe: out, sword, and to a sore purpose! Fortune, put them into my hand! This is the very description of their meeting-place; and the fellow dares not deceive me.

Exit

SCENE II. Before the Cave of Belarius.

Enter, from the cave, BELARIUS, GUIDERIUS, ARVIRAGUS, and IMOGEN

BELARIUS
[To IMOGEN] You are not well: remain here in the cave;
We'll come to you after hunting.

ARVIRAGUS
[To IMOGEN] Brother, stay here
Are we not brothers?

IMOGEN
So man and man should be;
But clay and clay differs in dignity,
Whose dust is both alike. I am very sick.

GUIDERIUS
Go you to hunting; I'll abide with him.

IMOGEN
So sick I am not, yet I am not well;
But not so citizen a wanton as
To seem to die ere sick: so please you, leave me;
Stick to your journal course: the breach of custom
Is breach of all. I am ill, but your being by me
Cannot amend me; society is no comfort

To one not sociable: I am not very sick,
Since I can reason of it. Pray you, trust me here:
I'll rob none but myself; and let me die,
Stealing so poorly.

GUIDERIUS
I love thee; I have spoke it
How much the quantity, the weight as much,
As I do love my father.

BELARIUS
What! how! how!

ARVIRAGUS
If it be sin to say so, I yoke me
In my good brother's fault: I know not why
I love this youth; and I have heard you say,
Love's reason's without reason: the bier at door,
And a demand who is't shall die, I'd say
'My father, not this youth.'

BELARIUS
[Aside] O noble strain!
O worthiness of nature! breed of greatness!
Cowards father cowards and base things sire base:
Nature hath meal and bran, contempt and grace.
I'm not their father; yet who this should be,
Doth miracle itself, loved before me.
'Tis the ninth hour o' the morn.

ARVIRAGUS
Brother, farewell.

IMOGEN
I wish ye sport.

ARVIRAGUS
You health. So please you, sir.

IMOGEN
[Aside] These are kind creatures. Gods, what lies
I have heard!
Our courtiers say all's savage but at court:
Experience, O, thou disprovest report!
The imperious seas breed monsters, for the dish
Poor tributary rivers as sweet fish.
I am sick still; heart-sick. Pisanio,
I'll now taste of thy drug.

Swallows some

GUIDERIUS
I could not stir him:
He said he was gentle, but unfortunate;
Dishonestly afflicted, but yet honest.

ARVIRAGUS
Thus did he answer me: yet said, hereafter
I might know more.

BELARIUS
To the field, to the field!
We'll leave you for this time: go in and rest.

ARVIRAGUS
We'll not be long away.

BELARIUS
Pray, be not sick,
For you must be our housewife.

IMOGEN
Well or ill,
I am bound to you.

BELARIUS
And shalt be ever.

Exit IMOGEN, to the cave

This youth, how'er distress'd, appears he hath had
Good ancestors.

ARVIRAGUS
How angel-like he sings!

GUIDERIUS
But his neat cookery! he cut our roots
In characters,
And sauced our broths, as Juno had been sick
And he her dieter.

ARVIRAGUS
Nobly he yokes
A smiling with a sigh, as if the sigh
Was that it was, for not being such a smile;
The smile mocking the sigh, that it would fly
From so divine a temple, to commix
With winds that sailors rail at.

GUIDERIUS

I do note
That grief and patience, rooted in him both,
Mingle their spurs together.

ARVIRAGUS
Grow, patience!
And let the stinking elder, grief, untwine
His perishing root with the increasing vine!

BELARIUS
It is great morning. Come, away!—
Who's there?

Enter CLOTEN

CLOTEN
I cannot find those runagates; that villain
Hath mock'd me. I am faint.

BELARIUS
'Those runagates!'
Means he not us? I partly know him: 'tis
Cloten, the son o' the queen. I fear some ambush.
I saw him not these many years, and yet
I know 'tis he. We are held as outlaws: hence!

GUIDERIUS
He is but one: you and my brother search
What companies are near: pray you, away;
Let me alone with him.

Exeunt BELARIUS and ARVIRAGUS

CLOTEN
Soft! What are you
That fly me thus? some villain mountaineers?
I have heard of such. What slave art thou?

GUIDERIUS
A thing
More slavish did I ne'er than answering
A slave without a knock.

CLOTEN
Thou art a robber,
A law-breaker, a villain: yield thee, thief.

GUIDERIUS
To who? to thee? What art thou? Have not I
An arm as big as thine? a heart as big?
Thy words, I grant, are bigger, for I wear not

My dagger in my mouth. Say what thou art,
Why I should yield to thee?

CLOTEN
Thou villain base,
Know'st me not by my clothes?

GUIDERIUS
No, nor thy tailor, rascal,
Who is thy grandfather: he made those clothes,
Which, as it seems, make thee.

CLOTEN
Thou precious varlet,
My tailor made them not.

GUIDERIUS
Hence, then, and thank
The man that gave them thee. Thou art some fool;
I am loath to beat thee.

CLOTEN
Thou injurious thief,
Hear but my name, and tremble.

GUIDERIUS
What's thy name?

CLOTEN
Cloten, thou villain.

GUIDERIUS
Cloten, thou double villain, be thy name,
I cannot tremble at it: were it Toad, or
Adder, Spider,
'Twould move me sooner.

CLOTEN
To thy further fear,
Nay, to thy mere confusion, thou shalt know
I am son to the queen.

GUIDERIUS
I am sorry for 't; not seeming
So worthy as thy birth.

CLOTEN
Art not afeard?

GUIDERIUS

Those that I reverence those I fear, the wise:
At fools I laugh, not fear them.

CLOTEN
Die the death:
When I have slain thee with my proper hand,
I'll follow those that even now fled hence,
And on the gates of Lud's-town set your heads:
Yield, rustic mountaineer.

Exeunt, fighting.

Re-enter BELARIUS and ARVIRAGUS

BELARIUS
No companies abroad?

ARVIRAGUS
None in the world: you did mistake him, sure.

BELARIUS
I cannot tell: long is it since I saw him,
But time hath nothing blurr'd those lines of favour
Which then he wore; the snatches in his voice,
And burst of speaking, were as his: I am absolute
'Twas very Cloten.

ARVIRAGUS
In this place we left them:
I wish my brother make good time with him,
You say he is so fell.

BELARIUS
Being scarce made up,
I mean, to man, he had not apprehension
Of roaring terrors; for the effect of judgment
Is oft the cause of fear. But, see, thy brother.

Re-enter GUIDERIUS, with CLOTEN'S head

GUIDERIUS
This Cloten was a fool, an empty purse;
There was no money in't: not Hercules
Could have knock'd out his brains, for he had none:
Yet I not doing this, the fool had borne
My head as I do his.

BELARIUS
What hast thou done?

GUIDERIUS

I am perfect what: cut off one Cloten's head,
Son to the queen, after his own report;
Who call'd me traitor, mountaineer, and swore
With his own single hand he'ld take us in
Displace our heads where—thank the gods!—they grow,
And set them on Lud's-town.

BELARIUS
We are all undone.

GUIDERIUS
Why, worthy father, what have we to lose,
But that he swore to take, our lives? The law
Protects not us: then why should we be tender
To let an arrogant piece of flesh threat us,
Play judge and executioner all himself,
For we do fear the law? What company
Discover you abroad?

BELARIUS
No single soul
Can we set eye on; but in all safe reason
He must have some attendants. Though his humour
Was nothing but mutation, ay, and that
From one bad thing to worse; not frenzy, not
Absolute madness could so far have raved
To bring him here alone; although perhaps
It may be heard at court that such as we
Cave here, hunt here, are outlaws, and in time
May make some stronger head; the which he hearing—
As it is like him—might break out, and swear
He'ld fetch us in; yet is't not probable
To come alone, either he so undertaking,
Or they so suffering: then on good ground we fear,
If we do fear this body hath a tail
More perilous than the head.

ARVIRAGUS
Let ordinance
Come as the gods foresay it: howsoe'er,
My brother hath done well.

BELARIUS
I had no mind
To hunt this day: the boy Fidele's sickness
Did make my way long forth.

GUIDERIUS
With his own sword,
Which he did wave against my throat, I have ta'en
His head from him: I'll throw't into the creek

Behind our rock; and let it to the sea,
And tell the fishes he's the queen's son, Cloten:
That's all I reck.

Exit

BELARIUS
I fear 'twill be revenged:
Would, Polydote, thou hadst not done't! though valour
Becomes thee well enough.

ARVIRAGUS
Would I had done't
So the revenge alone pursued me! Polydore,
I love thee brotherly, but envy much
Thou hast robb'd me of this deed: I would revenges,
That possible strength might meet, would seek us through
And put us to our answer.

BELARIUS
Well, 'tis done:
We'll hunt no more to-day, nor seek for danger
Where there's no profit. I prithee, to our rock;
You and Fidele play the cooks: I'll stay
Till hasty Polydote return, and bring him
To dinner presently.

ARVIRAGUS
Poor sick Fidele!
I'll weringly to him: to gain his colour
I'ld let a parish of such Clotens' blood,
And praise myself for charity.

Exit

BELARIUS
O thou goddess,
Thou divine Nature, how thyself thou blazon'st
In these two princely boys! They are as gentle
As zephyrs blowing below the violet,
Not wagging his sweet head; and yet as rough,
Their royal blood enchafed, as the rudest wind,
That by the top doth take the mountain pine,
And make him stoop to the vale. 'Tis wonder
That an invisible instinct should frame them
To royalty unlearn'd, honour untaught,
Civility not seen from other, valour
That wildly grows in them, but yields a crop
As if it had been sow'd. Yet still it's strange
What Cloten's being here to us portends,
Or what his death will bring us.

Re-enter GUIDERIUS

GUIDERIUS
Where's my brother?
I have sent Cloten's clotpoll down the stream,
In embassy to his mother: his body's hostage
For his return.

Solemn music

BELARIUS
My ingenious instrument!
Hark, Polydore, it sounds! But what occasion
Hath Cadwal now to give it motion? Hark!

GUIDERIUS
Is he at home?

BELARIUS
He went hence even now.

GUIDERIUS
What does he mean? since death of my dear'st mother
it did not speak before. All solemn things
Should answer solemn accidents. The matter?
Triumphs for nothing and lamenting toys
Is jollity for apes and grief for boys.
Is Cadwal mad?

BELARIUS
Look, here he comes,
And brings the dire occasion in his arms
Of what we blame him for.

Re-enter ARVIRAGUS, with IMOGEN, as dead, bearing her in his arms

ARVIRAGUS
The bird is dead
That we have made so much on. I had rather
Have skipp'd from sixteen years of age to sixty,
To have turn'd my leaping-time into a crutch,
Than have seen this.

GUIDERIUS
O sweetest, fairest lily!
My brother wears thee not the one half so well
As when thou grew'st thyself.

BELARIUS

O melancholy!
Who ever yet could sound thy bottom? find
The ooze, to show what coast thy sluggish crare
Might easiliest harbour in? Thou blessed thing!
Jove knows what man thou mightst have made; but I,
Thou diedst, a most rare boy, of melancholy.
How found you him?

ARVIRAGUS
Stark, as you see:
Thus smiling, as some fly hid tickled slumber,
Not as death's dart, being laugh'd at; his
right cheek
Reposing on a cushion.

GUIDERIUS
Where?

ARVIRAGUS
O' the floor;
His arms thus leagued: I thought he slept, and put
My clouted brogues from off my feet, whose rudeness
Answer'd my steps too loud.

GUIDERIUS
Why, he but sleeps:
If he be gone, he'll make his grave a bed;
With female fairies will his tomb be haunted,
And worms will not come to thee.

ARVIRAGUS
With fairest flowers
Whilst summer lasts and I live here, Fidele,
I'll sweeten thy sad grave: thou shalt not lack
The flower that's like thy face, pale primrose, nor
The azured harebell, like thy veins, no, nor
The leaf of eglantine, whom not to slander,
Out-sweeten'd not thy breath: the ruddock would,
With charitable bill,—O bill, sore-shaming
Those rich-left heirs that let their fathers lie
Without a monument!—bring thee all this;
Yea, and furr'd moss besides, when flowers are none,
To winter-ground thy corse.

GUIDERIUS
Prithee, have done;
And do not play in wench-like words with that
Which is so serious. Let us bury him,
And not protract with admiration what
Is now due debt. To the grave!

ARVIRAGUS
Say, where shall's lay him?

GUIDERIUS
By good Euriphile, our mother.

ARVIRAGUS
Be't so:
And let us, Polydore, though now our voices
Have got the mannish crack, sing him to the ground,
As once our mother; use like note and words,
Save that Euriphile must be Fidele.

GUIDERIUS
Cadwal,
I cannot sing: I'll weep, and word it with thee;
For notes of sorrow out of tune are worse
Than priests and fanes that lie.

ARVIRAGUS
We'll speak it, then.

BELARIUS
Great griefs, I see, medicine the less; for Cloten
Is quite forgot. He was a queen's son, boys;
And though he came our enemy, remember
He was paid for that: though mean and mighty, rotting
Together, have one dust, yet reverence,
That angel of the world, doth make distinction
Of place 'tween high and low. Our foe was princely
And though you took his life, as being our foe,
Yet bury him as a prince.

GUIDERIUS
Pray You, fetch him hither.
Thersites' body is as good as Ajax',
When neither are alive.

ARVIRAGUS
If you'll go fetch him,
We'll say our song the whilst. Brother, begin.

Exit BELARIUS

GUIDERIUS
Nay, Cadwal, we must lay his head to the east;
My father hath a reason for't.

ARVIRAGUS
'Tis true.

GUIDERIUS
Come on then, and remove him.

ARVIRAGUS
So. Begin.

SONG

GUIDERIUS
Fear no more the heat o' the sun,
Nor the furious winter's rages;
Thou thy worldly task hast done,
Home art gone, and ta'en thy wages:
Golden lads and girls all must,
As chimney-sweepers, come to dust.

ARVIRAGUS
Fear no more the frown o' the great;
Thou art past the tyrant's stroke;
Care no more to clothe and eat;
To thee the reed is as the oak:
The sceptre, learning, physic, must
All follow this, and come to dust.

GUIDERIUS
Fear no more the lightning flash,

ARVIRAGUS
Nor the all-dreaded thunder-stone;

GUIDERIUS
Fear not slander, censure rash;

ARVIRAGUS
Thou hast finish'd joy and moan:

GUIDERIUS ARVIRAGUS
All lovers young, all lovers must
Consign to thee, and come to dust.

GUIDERIUS
No exorciser harm thee!

ARVIRAGUS
Nor no witchcraft charm thee!

GUIDERIUS
Ghost unlaid forbear thee!

ARVIRAGUS
Nothing ill come near thee!

GUIDERIUS ARVIRAGUS
Quiet consummation have;
And renowned be thy grave!

Re-enter BELARIUS, with the body of CLOTEN

GUIDERIUS
We have done our obsequies: come, lay him down.

BELARIUS
Here's a few flowers; but 'bout midnight, more:
The herbs that have on them cold dew o' the night
Are strewings fitt'st for graves. Upon their faces.
You were as flowers, now wither'd: even so
These herblets shall, which we upon you strew.
Come on, away: apart upon our knees.
The ground that gave them first has them again:
Their pleasures here are past, so is their pain.

Exeunt BELARIUS, GUIDERIUS, and ARVIRAGUS

IMOGEN
[Awaking] Yes, sir, to Milford-Haven; which is the way?—
I thank you.—By yond bush?—Pray, how far thither?
'Ods pittikins! can it be six mile yet?—
I have gone all night. 'Faith, I'll lie down and sleep.
But, soft! no bedfellow!—O god s and goddesses!

Seeing the body of CLOTEN

These flowers are like the pleasures of the world;
This bloody man, the care on't. I hope I dream;
For so I thought I was a cave-keeper,
And cook to honest creatures: but 'tis not so;
'Twas but a bolt of nothing, shot at nothing,
Which the brain makes of fumes: our very eyes
Are sometimes like our judgments, blind. Good faith,
I tremble stiff with fear: but if there be
Yet left in heaven as small a drop of pity
As a wren's eye, fear'd gods, a part of it!
The dream's here still: even when I wake, it is
Without me, as within me; not imagined, felt.
A headless man! The garments of Posthumus!
I know the shape of's leg: this is his hand;
His foot Mercurial; his Martial thigh;
The brawns of Hercules: but his Jovial face
Murder in heaven?—How!—'Tis gone. Pisanio,
All curses madded Hecuba gave the Greeks,
And mine to boot, be darted on thee! Thou,
Conspired with that irregulous devil, Cloten,

Hast here cut off my lord. To write and read
Be henceforth treacherous! Damn'd Pisanio
Hath with his forged letters,—damn'd Pisanio—
From this most bravest vessel of the world
Struck the main-top! O Posthumus! alas,
Where is thy head? where's that? Ay me! where's that?
Pisanio might have kill'd thee at the heart,
And left this head on. How should this be? Pisanio?
'Tis he and Cloten: malice and lucre in them
Have laid this woe here. O, 'tis pregnant, pregnant!
The drug he gave me, which he said was precious
And cordial to me, have I not found it
Murderous to the senses? That confirms it home:
This is Pisanio's deed, and Cloten's: O!
Give colour to my pale cheek with thy blood,
That we the horrider may seem to those
Which chance to find us: O, my lord, my lord!

Falls on the body
Enter LUCIUS, a CAPTAIN and other OFFICERS, and a SOOTHSAYER

CAPTAIN
To them the legions garrison'd in Gailia,
After your will, have cross'd the sea, attending
You here at Milford-Haven with your ships:
They are in readiness.

CAIUS LUCIUS
But what from Rome?

CAPTAIN
The senate hath stirr'd up the confiners
And gentlemen of Italy, most willing spirits,
That promise noble service: and they come
Under the conduct of bold Iachimo,
Syenna's brother.

CAIUS LUCIUS
When expect you them?

Captain
With the next benefit o' the wind.

CAIUS LUCIUS
This forwardness
Makes our hopes fair. Command our present numbers
Be muster'd; bid the captains look to't. Now, sir,
What have you dream'd of late of this war's purpose?

Soothsayer

Last night the very gods show'd me a vision—
I fast and pray'd for their intelligence—thus:
I saw Jove's bird, the Roman eagle, wing'd
From the spongy south to this part of the west,
There vanish'd in the sunbeams: which portends—
Unless my sins abuse my divination—
Success to the Roman host.

CAIUS LUCIUS
Dream often so,
And never false. Soft, ho! what trunk is here
Without his top? The ruin speaks that sometime
It was a worthy building. How! a page!
Or dead, or sleeping on him? But dead rather;
For nature doth abhor to make his bed
With the defunct, or sleep upon the dead.
Let's see the boy's face.

CAPTAIN
He's alive, my lord.

CAIUS LUCIUS
He'll then instruct us of this body. Young one,
Inform us of thy fortunes, for it seems
They crave to be demanded. Who is this
Thou makest thy bloody pillow? Or who was he
That, otherwise than noble nature did,
Hath alter'd that good picture? What's thy interest
In this sad wreck? How came it? Who is it?
What art thou?

IMOGEN
I am nothing: or if not,
Nothing to be were better. This was my master,
A very valiant Briton and a good,
That here by mountaineers lies slain. Alas!
There is no more such masters: I may wander
From east to occident, cry out for service,
Try many, all good, serve truly, never
Find such another master.

CAIUS LUCIUS
'Lack, good youth!
Thou movest no less with thy complaining than
Thy master in bleeding: say his name, good friend.

IMOGEN
Richard du Champ.

Aside

If I do lie and do
No harm by it, though the gods hear, I hope
They'll pardon it.—Say you, sir?

CAIUS LUCIUS
Thy name?

IMOGEN
Fidele, sir.

CAIUS LUCIUS
Thou dost approve thyself the very same:
Thy name well fits thy faith, thy faith thy name.
Wilt take thy chance with me? I will not say
Thou shalt be so well master'd, but, be sure,
No less beloved. The Roman emperor's letters,
Sent by a consul to me, should not sooner
Than thine own worth prefer thee: go with me.

IMOGEN
I'll follow, sir. But first, an't please the gods,
I'll hide my master from the flies, as deep
As these poor pickaxes can dig; and when
With wild wood-leaves and weeds I ha' strew'd his grave,
And on it said a century of prayers,
Such as I can, twice o'er, I'll weep and sigh;
And leaving so his service, follow you,
So please you entertain me.

CAIUS LUCIUS
Ay, good youth!
And rather father thee than master thee.
My friends,
The boy hath taught us manly duties: let us
Find out the prettiest daisied plot we can,
And make him with our pikes and partisans
A grave: come, arm him. Boy, he is preferr'd
By thee to us, and he shall be interr'd
As soldiers can. Be cheerful; wipe thine eyes
Some falls are means the happier to arise.

Exeunt

SCENE III. A Room in Cymbeline's Palace.

Enter CYMBELINE, Lords, PISANIO, and ATTENDANTS

CYMBELINE
Again; and bring me word how 'tis with her.

Exit an ATTENDANT

A fever with the absence of her son,
A madness, of which her life's in danger. Heavens,
How deeply you at once do touch me! Imogen,
The great part of my comfort, gone; my queen
Upon a desperate bed, and in a time
When fearful wars point at me; her son gone,
So needful for this present: it strikes me, past
The hope of comfort. But for thee, fellow,
Who needs must know of her departure and
Dost seem so ignorant, we'll enforce it from thee
By a sharp torture.

PISANIO
Sir, my life is yours;
I humbly set it at your will; but, for my mistress,
I nothing know where she remains, why gone,
Nor when she purposes return. Beseech your highness,
Hold me your loyal servant.

FIRST LORD
Good my liege,
The day that she was missing he was here:
I dare be bound he's true and shall perform
All parts of his subjection loyally. For Cloten,
There wants no diligence in seeking him,
And will, no doubt, be found.

CYMBELINE
The time is troublesome.

To PISANIO

We'll slip you for a season; but our jealousy
Does yet depend.

FIRST LORD
So please your majesty,
The Roman legions, all from Gallia drawn,
Are landed on your coast, with a supply
Of Roman gentlemen, by the senate sent.

CYMBELINE
Now for the counsel of my son and queen!
I am amazed with matter.

FIRST LORD
Good my liege,
Your preparation can affront no less

Than what you hear of: come more, for more you're ready:
The want is but to put those powers in motion
That long to move.

CYMBELINE
I thank you. Let's withdraw;
And meet the time as it seeks us. We fear not
What can from Italy annoy us; but
We grieve at chances here. Away!

Exeunt all but PISANIO

PISANIO
I heard no letter from my master since
I wrote him Imogen was slain: 'tis strange:
Nor hear I from my mistress who did promise
To yield me often tidings: neither know I
What is betid to Cloten; but remain
Perplex'd in all. The heavens still must work.
Wherein I am false I am honest; not true, to be true.
These present wars shall find I love my country,
Even to the note o' the king, or I'll fall in them.
All other doubts, by time let them be clear'd:
Fortune brings in some boats that are not steer'd.

Exit

SCENE IV. Wales: Before the Cave of Belarius.

Enter BELARIUS, GUIDERIUS, and ARVIRAGUS.

GUIDERIUS
The noise is round about us.

BELARIUS
Let us from it.

ARVIRAGUS
What pleasure, sir, find we in life, to lock it
From action and adventure?

GUIDERIUS
Nay, what hope
Have we in hiding us? This way, the Romans
Must or for Britons slay us, or receive us
For barbarous and unnatural revolts
During their use, and slay us after.

BELARIUS

Sons,
We'll higher to the mountains; there secure us.
To the king's party there's no going: newness
Of Cloten's death—we being not known, not muster'd
Among the bands—may drive us to a render
Where we have lived, and so extort from's that
Which we have done, whose answer would be death
Drawn on with torture.

GUIDERIUS
This is, sir, a doubt
In such a time nothing becoming you,
Nor satisfying us.

ARVIRAGUS
It is not likely
That when they hear the Roman horses neigh,
Behold their quarter'd fires, have both their eyes
And ears so cloy'd importantly as now,
That they will waste their time upon our note,
To know from whence we are.

BELARIUS
O, I am known
Of many in the army: many years,
Though Cloten then but young, you see, not wore him
From my remembrance. And, besides, the king
Hath not deserved my service nor your loves;
Who find in my exile the want of breeding,
The certainty of this hard life; aye hopeless
To have the courtesy your cradle promised,
But to be still hot summer's tamings and
The shrinking slaves of winter.

GUIDERIUS
Than be so
Better to cease to be. Pray, sir, to the army:
I and my brother are not known; yourself
So out of thought, and thereto so o'ergrown,
Cannot be question'd.

ARVIRAGUS
By this sun that shines,
I'll thither: what thing is it that I never
Did see man die! scarce ever look'd on blood,
But that of coward hares, hot goats, and venison!
Never bestrid a horse, save one that had
A rider like myself, who ne'er wore rowel
Nor iron on his heel! I am ashamed
To look upon the holy sun, to have

The benefit of his blest beams, remaining
So long a poor unknown.

GUIDERIUS
By heavens, I'll go:
If you will bless me, sir, and give me leave,
I'll take the better care, but if you will not,
The hazard therefore due fall on me by
The hands of Romans!

ARVIRAGUS
So say I amen.

BELARIUS
No reason I, since of your lives you set
So slight a valuation, should reserve
My crack'd one to more care. Have with you, boys!
If in your country wars you chance to die,
That is my bed too, lads, an there I'll lie:
Lead, lead.

Aside

The time seems long; their blood
thinks scorn,
Till it fly out and show them princes born.

Exeunt

ACT V

SCENE I. Britain. The Roman Camp.

Enter POSTHUMUS, with a bloody handkerchief

POSTHUMUS LEONATUS
Yea, bloody cloth, I'll keep thee, for I wish'd
Thou shouldst be colour'd thus. You married ones,
If each of you should take this course, how many
Must murder wives much better than themselves
For wrying but a little! O Pisanio!
Every good servant does not all commands:
No bond but to do just ones. Gods! if you
Should have ta'en vengeance on my faults, I never
Had lived to put on this: so had you saved
The noble Imogen to repent, and struck
Me, wretch more worth your vengeance. But, alack,
You snatch some hence for little faults; that's love,

To have them fall no more: you some permit
To second ills with ills, each elder worse,
And make them dread it, to the doers' thrift.
But Imogen is your own: do your best wills,
And make me blest to obey! I am brought hither
Among the Italian gentry, and to fight
Against my lady's kingdom: 'tis enough
That, Britain, I have kill'd thy mistress; peace!
I'll give no wound to thee. Therefore, good heavens,
Hear patiently my purpose: I'll disrobe me
Of these Italian weeds and suit myself
As does a Briton peasant: so I'll fight
Against the part I come with; so I'll die
For thee, O Imogen, even for whom my life
Is every breath a death; and thus, unknown,
Pitied nor hated, to the face of peril
Myself I'll dedicate. Let me make men know
More valour in me than my habits show.
Gods, put the strength o' the Leonati in me!
To shame the guise o' the world, I will begin
The fashion, less without and more within.

Exit

SCENE II. Field of Battle Between the British and Roman Camps.

Enter, from one side, LUCIUS, IACHIMO, and the Roman Army: from the other side, the British Army; POSTHUMUS LEONATUS following, like a poor soldier. They march over and go out.

Then enter again, in skirmish, IACHIMO and POSTHUMUS LEONATUS he vanquisheth and disarmeth IACHIMO, and then leaves him

IACHIMO
The heaviness and guilt within my bosom
Takes off my manhood: I have belied a lady,
The princess of this country, and the air on't
Revengingly enfeebles me; or could this carl,
A very drudge of nature's, have subdued me
In my profession? Knighthoods and honours, borne
As I wear mine, are titles but of scorn.
If that thy gentry, Britain, go before
This lout as he exceeds our lords, the odds
Is that we scarce are men and you are gods.

Exit

The battle continues; the Britons fly; CYMBELINE is taken: then enter, to his rescue, BELARIUS, GUIDERIUS, and ARVIRAGUS

BELARIUS
Stand, stand! We have the advantage of the ground;
The lane is guarded: nothing routs us but
The villany of our fears.

GUIDERIUS ARVIRAGUS
Stand, stand, and fight!

Re-enter POSTHUMUS LEONATUS, and seconds the Britons: they rescue CYMBELINE, and exeunt.

Then re-enter LUCIUS, and IACHIMO, with IMOGEN

CAIUS LUCIUS
Away, boy, from the troops, and save thyself;
For friends kill friends, and the disorder's such
As war were hoodwink'd.

IACHIMO
'Tis their fresh supplies.

CAIUS LUCIUS
It is a day turn'd strangely: or betimes
Let's reinforce, or fly.

Exeunt

SCENE III. Another Part of the Field.

Enter POSTHUMUS LEONATUS and a British LORD

LORD
Camest thou from where they made the stand?

POSTHUMUS LEONATUS
I did.
Though you, it seems, come from the fliers.

LORD
I did.

POSTHUMUS LEONATUS
No blame be to you, sir; for all was lost,
But that the heavens fought: the king himself
Of his wings destitute, the army broken,
And but the backs of Britons seen, all flying
Through a straight lane; the enemy full-hearted,
Lolling the tongue with slaughtering, having work
More plentiful than tools to do't, struck down
Some mortally, some slightly touch'd, some falling

Merely through fear; that the straight pass was damm'd
With dead men hurt behind, and cowards living
To die with lengthen'd shame.

LORD
Where was this lane?

POSTHUMUS LEONATUS
Close by the battle, ditch'd, and wall'd with turf;
Which gave advantage to an ancient soldier,
An honest one, I warrant; who deserved
So long a breeding as his white beard came to,
In doing this for's country: athwart the lane,
He, with two striplings-lads more like to run
The country base than to commit such slaughter
With faces fit for masks, or rather fairer
Than those for preservation cased, or shame—
Made good the passage; cried to those that fled,
'Our Britain s harts die flying, not our men:
To darkness fleet souls that fly backwards. Stand;
Or we are Romans and will give you that
Like beasts which you shun beastly, and may save,
But to look back in frown: stand, stand.'
These three,
Three thousand confident, in act as many—
For three performers are the file when all
The rest do nothing—with this word 'Stand, stand,'
Accommodated by the place, more charming
With their own nobleness, which could have turn'd
A distaff to a lance, gilded pale looks,
Part shame, part spirit renew'd; that some, turn'd coward
But by example—O, a sin in war,
Damn'd in the first beginners!—gan to look
The way that they did, and to grin like lions
Upon the pikes o' the hunters. Then began
A stop i' the chaser, a retire, anon
A rout, confusion thick; forthwith they fly
Chickens, the way which they stoop'd eagles; slaves,
The strides they victors made: and now our cowards,
Like fragments in hard voyages, became
The life o' the need: having found the backdoor open
Of the unguarded hearts, heavens, how they wound!
Some slain before; some dying; some their friends
O'er borne i' the former wave: ten, chased by one,
Are now each one the slaughter-man of twenty:
Those that would die or ere resist are grown
The mortal bugs o' the field.

LORD
This was strange chance
A narrow lane, an old man, and two boys.

POSTHUMUS LEONATUS
Nay, do not wonder at it: you are made
Rather to wonder at the things you hear
Than to work any. Will you rhyme upon't,
And vent it for a mockery? Here is one:
'Two boys, an old man twice a boy, a lane,
Preserved the Britons, was the Romans' bane.'

LORD
Nay, be not angry, sir.

POSTHUMUS LEONATUS
'Lack, to what end?
Who dares not stand his foe, I'll be his friend;
For if he'll do as he is made to do,
I know he'll quickly fly my friendship too.
You have put me into rhyme.

LORD
Farewell; you're angry.

POSTHUMUS LEONATUS
Still going?

Exit LORD

This is a lord! O noble misery,
To be i' the field, and ask 'what news?' of me!
To-day how many would have given their honours
To have saved their carcasses! took heel to do't,
And yet died too! I, in mine own woe charm'd,
Could not find death where I did hear him groan,
Nor feel him where he struck: being an ugly monster,
'Tis strange he hides him in fresh cups, soft beds,
Sweet words; or hath more ministers than we
That draw his knives i' the war. Well, I will find him
For being now a favourer to the Briton,
No more a Briton, I have resumed again
The part I came in: fight I will no more,
But yield me to the veriest hind that shall
Once touch my shoulder. Great the slaughter is
Here made by the Roman; great the answer be
Britons must take. For me, my ransom's death;
On either side I come to spend my breath;
Which neither here I'll keep nor bear again,
But end it by some means for Imogen.

Enter two British CAPTAINS and SOLDIERS

FIRST CAPTAIN

Great Jupiter be praised! Lucius is taken.
'Tis thought the old man and his sons were angels.

SECOND CAPTAIN
There was a fourth man, in a silly habit,
That gave the affront with them.

FIRST CAPTAIN
So 'tis reported:
But none of 'em can be found. Stand! who's there?

POSTHUMUS LEONATUS
A Roman,
Who had not now been drooping here, if seconds
Had answer'd him.

SECOND CAPTAIN
Lay hands on him; a dog!
A leg of Rome shall not return to tell
What crows have peck'd them here. He brags his service
As if he were of note: bring him to the king.

Enter CYMBELINE, BELARIUS, GUIDERIUS, ARVIRAGUS, PISANIO, Soldiers, Attendants, and Roman Captives. The Captains present POSTHUMUS LEONATUS to CYMBELINE, who delivers him over to a Gaoler: then exeunt omnes

SCENE IV. A British Prison.

Enter POSTHUMUS LEONATUS and two GAOLERS

FIRST GAOLER
You shall not now be stol'n, you have locks upon you;
So graze as you find pasture.

SECOND GAOLER
Ay, or a stomach.

Exeunt GAOLERS

POSTHUMUS LEONATUS
Most welcome, bondage! for thou art away,
think, to liberty: yet am I better
Than one that's sick o' the gout; since he had rather
Groan so in perpetuity than be cured
By the sure physician, death, who is the key
To unbar these locks. My conscience, thou art fetter'd
More than my shanks and wrists: you good gods, give me
The penitent instrument to pick that bolt,
Then, free for ever! Is't enough I am sorry?

So children temporal fathers do appease;
Gods are more full of mercy. Must I repent?
I cannot do it better than in gyves,
Desired more than constrain'd: to satisfy,
If of my freedom 'tis the main part, take
No stricter render of me than my all.
I know you are more clement than vile men,
Who of their broken debtors take a third,
A sixth, a tenth, letting them thrive again
On their abatement: that's not my desire:
For Imogen's dear life take mine; and though
'Tis not so dear, yet 'tis a life; you coin'd it:
'Tween man and man they weigh not every stamp;
Though light, take pieces for the figure's sake:
You rather mine, being yours: and so, great powers,
If you will take this audit, take this life,
And cancel these cold bonds. O Imogen!
I'll speak to thee in silence.

Sleeps

Solemn music.

Enter, as in an apparition, SICILIUS LEONATUS, father to Posthumus Leonatus, an old man, attired like a warrior; leading in his hand an ancient matron, his wife, and mother to Posthumus Leonatus, with music before them: then, after other music, follow the two young Leonati, brothers to Posthumus Leonatus, with wounds as they died in the wars. They circle POSTHUMUS LEONATUS round, as he lies sleeping

SICILIUS LEONATUS
No more, thou thunder-master, show
Thy spite on mortal flies:
With Mars fall out, with Juno chide,
That thy adulteries
Rates and revenges.
Hath my poor boy done aught but well,
Whose face I never saw?
I died whilst in the womb he stay'd
Attending nature's law:
Whose father then, as men report
Thou orphans' father art,
Thou shouldst have been, and shielded him
From this earth-vexing smart.

MOTHER
Lucina lent not me her aid,
But took me in my throes;
That from me was Posthumus ript,
Came crying 'mongst his foes,
A thing of pity!

SICILIUS LEONATUS
Great nature, like his ancestry,
Moulded the stuff so fair,
That he deserved the praise o' the world,
As great Sicilius' heir.

FIRST BROTHER
When once he was mature for man,
In Britain where was he
That could stand up his parallel;
Or fruitful object be
In eye of Imogen, that best
Could deem his dignity?

MOTHER
With marriage wherefore was he mock'd,
To be exiled, and thrown
From Leonati seat, and cast
From her his dearest one,
Sweet Imogen?

SICILIUS LEONATUS
Why did you suffer Iachimo,
Slight thing of Italy,
To taint his nobler heart and brain
With needless jealosy;
And to become the geck and scorn
O' th' other's villany?

SECOND BROTHER
For this from stiller seats we came,
Our parents and us twain,
That striking in our country's cause
Fell bravely and were slain,
Our fealty and Tenantius' right
With honour to maintain.

FIRST BROTHER
Like hardiment Posthumus hath
To Cymbeline perform'd:
Then, Jupiter, thou king of gods,
Why hast thou thus adjourn'd
The graces for his merits due,
Being all to dolours turn'd?

SICILIUS LEONATUS
Thy crystal window ope; look out;
No longer exercise
Upon a valiant race thy harsh
And potent injuries.

MOTHER
Since, Jupiter, our son is good,
Take off his miseries.

SICILIUS LEONATUS
Peep through thy marble mansion; help;
Or we poor ghosts will cry
To the shining synod of the rest
Against thy deity.

FIRST BROTHER/SECOND BROTHER
Help, Jupiter; or we appeal,
And from thy justice fly.

JUPITER descends in thunder and lightning, sitting upon an eagle: he throws a thunderbolt. The Apparitions fall on their knees

JUPITER
No more, you petty spirits of region low,
Offend our hearing; hush! How dare you ghosts
Accuse the thunderer, whose bolt, you know,
Sky-planted batters all rebelling coasts?
Poor shadows of Elysium, hence, and rest
Upon your never-withering banks of flowers:
Be not with mortal accidents opprest;
No care of yours it is; you know 'tis ours.
Whom best I love I cross; to make my gift,
The more delay'd, delighted. Be content;
Your low-laid son our godhead will uplift:
His comforts thrive, his trials well are spent.
Our Jovial star reign'd at his birth, and in
Our temple was he married. Rise, and fade.
He shall be lord of lady Imogen,
And happier much by his affliction made.
This tablet lay upon his breast, wherein
Our pleasure his full fortune doth confine:
and so, away: no further with your din
Express impatience, lest you stir up mine.
Mount, eagle, to my palace crystalline.

Ascends

SICILIUS LEONATUS
He came in thunder; his celestial breath
Was sulphurous to smell: the holy eagle
Stoop'd as to foot us: his ascension is
More sweet than our blest fields: his royal bird
Prunes the immortal wing and cloys his beak,
As when his god is pleased.

ALL

Thanks, Jupiter!

SICILIUS LEONATUS
The marble pavement closes, he is enter'd
His radiant roof. Away! and, to be blest,
Let us with care perform his great behest.

The Apparitions vanish

POSTHUMUS LEONATUS
[Waking] Sleep, thou hast been a grandsire, and begot
A father to me; and thou hast created
A mother and two brothers: but, O scorn!
Gone! they went hence so soon as they were born:
And so I am awake. Poor wretches that depend
On greatness' favour dream as I have done,
Wake and find nothing. But, alas, I swerve:
Many dream not to find, neither deserve,
And yet are steep'd in favours: so am I,
That have this golden chance and know not why.
What fairies haunt this ground? A book? O rare one!
Be not, as is our fangled world, a garment
Nobler than that it covers: let thy effects
So follow, to be most unlike our courtiers,
As good as promise.

Reads

'When as a lion's whelp shall, to himself unknown, without seeking find, and be embraced by a piece of tender air; and when from a stately cedar shall be lopped branches, which, being dead many years, shall after revive, be jointed to the old stock and freshly grow; then shall Posthumus end his miseries, Britain be fortunate and flourish in peace and plenty.' 'Tis still a dream, or else such stuff as madmen Tongue and brain not; either both or nothing; Or senseless speaking or a speaking such As sense cannot untie. Be what it is, The action of my life is like it, which I'll keep, if but for sympathy.

Re-enter FIRST GAOLER

FIRST GAOLER
Come, sir, are you ready for death?

POSTHUMUS LEONATUS
Over-roasted rather; ready long ago.

FIRST GAOLER
Hanging is the word, sir: if you be ready for that, you are well cooked.

POSTHUMUS LEONATUS
So, if I prove a good repast to the spectators, the dish pays the shot.

FIRST GAOLER

A heavy reckoning for you, sir. But the comfort is, you shall be called to no more payments, fear no more tavern-bills; which are often the sadness of parting, as the procuring of mirth: you come in flint for want of meat, depart reeling with too much drink; sorry that you have paid too much, and sorry that you are paid too much; purse and brain both empty; the brain the heavier for being too light, the purse too light, being drawn of heaviness: of this contradiction you shall now be quit. O, the charity of a penny cord! It sums up thousands in a trice: you have no true debitor and creditor but it; of what's past, is, and to come, the discharge: your neck, sir, is pen, book and counters; so the acquittance follows.

POSTHUMUS LEONATUS
I am merrier to die than thou art to live.

FIRST GAOLER
Indeed, sir, he that sleeps feels not the tooth-ache: but a man that were to sleep your sleep, and a hangman to help him to bed, I think he would change places with his officer; for, look you, sir, you know not which way you shall go.

POSTHUMUS LEONATUS
Yes, indeed do I, fellow.

FIRST GAOLER
Your death has eyes in 's head then; I have not seen him so pictured: you must either be directed by some that take upon them to know, or do take upon yourself that which I am sure you do not know, or jump the after inquiry on your own peril: and how you shall speed in your journey's end, I think you'll never return to tell one.

POSTHUMUS LEONATUS
I tell thee, fellow, there are none want eyes to direct them the way I am going, but such as wink and will not use them.

FIRST GAOLER
What an infinite mock is this, that a man should have the best use of eyes to see the way of blindness! I am sure hanging's the way of winking.

Enter a MESSENGER

MESSENGER
Knock off his manacles; bring your prisoner to the king.

POSTHUMUS LEONATUS
Thou bring'st good news; I am called to be made free.

FIRST GAOLER
I'll be hang'd then.

POSTHUMUS LEONATUS
Thou shalt be then freer than a gaoler; no bolts for the dead.

Exeunt POSTHUMUS LEONATUS and MESSENGER

FIRST GAOLER

Unless a man would marry a gallows and beget young gibbets, I never saw one so prone. Yet, on my conscience, there are verier knaves desire to live, for all he be a Roman: and there be some of them too that die against their wills; so should I, if I were one. I would we were all of one mind, and one mind good; O, there were desolation of gaolers and gallowses! I speak against my present profit, but my wish hath a preferment in 't.

Exeunt

SCENE V. Cymbeline's Tent.

Enter CYMBELINE, BELARIUS, GUIDERIUS, ARVIRAGUS, PISANIO, LORDS, OFFICERS, and ATTENDANTS

CYMBELINE
Stand by my side, you whom the gods have made
Preservers of my throne. Woe is my heart
That the poor soldier that so richly fought,
Whose rags shamed gilded arms, whose naked breast
Stepp'd before larges of proof, cannot be found:
He shall be happy that can find him, if
Our grace can make him so.

BELARIUS
I never saw
Such noble fury in so poor a thing;
Such precious deeds in one that promises nought
But beggary and poor looks.

CYMBELINE
No tidings of him?

PISANIO
He hath been search'd among the dead and living,
But no trace of him.

CYMBELINE
To my grief, I am
The heir of his reward;

To BELARIUS, GUIDERIUS, and ARVIRAGUS

Which I will add
To you, the liver, heart and brain of Britain,
By whom I grant she lives. 'Tis now the time
To ask of whence you are. Report it.

BELARIUS
Sir,
In Cambria are we born, and gentlemen:

Further to boast were neither true nor modest,
Unless I add, we are honest.

CYMBELINE
Bow your knees.
Arise my knights o' the battle: I create you
Companions to our person and will fit you
With dignities becoming your estates.

Enter CORNELIUS and Ladies

There's business in these faces. Why so sadly
Greet you our victory? you look like Romans,
And not o' the court of Britain.

CORNELIUS
Hail, great king!
To sour your happiness, I must report
The queen is dead.

CYMBELINE
Who worse than a physician
Would this report become? But I consider,
By medicine life may be prolong'd, yet death
Will seize the doctor too. How ended she?

CORNELIUS
With horror, madly dying, like her life,
Which, being cruel to the world, concluded
Most cruel to herself. What she confess'd
I will report, so please you: these her women
Can trip me, if I err; who with wet cheeks
Were present when she finish'd.

CYMBELINE
Prithee, say.

CORNELIUS
First, she confess'd she never loved you, only
Affected greatness got by you, not you:
Married your royalty, was wife to your place;
Abhorr'd your person.

CYMBELINE
She alone knew this;
And, but she spoke it dying, I would not
Believe her lips in opening it. Proceed.

CORNELIUS
Your daughter, whom she bore in hand to love
With such integrity, she did confess

Was as a scorpion to her sight; whose life,
But that her flight prevented it, she had
Ta'en off by poison.

CYMBELINE
O most delicate fiend!
Who is 't can read a woman? Is there more?

CORNELIUS
More, sir, and worse. She did confess she had
For you a mortal mineral; which, being took,
Should by the minute feed on life and lingering
By inches waste you: in which time she purposed,
By watching, weeping, tendance, kissing, to
O'ercome you with her show, and in time,
When she had fitted you with her craft, to work
Her son into the adoption of the crown:
But, failing of her end by his strange absence,
Grew shameless-desperate; open'd, in despite
Of heaven and men, her purposes; repented
The evils she hatch'd were not effected; so
Despairing died.

CYMBELINE
Heard you all this, her women?

First Lady
We did, so please your highness.

CYMBELINE
Mine eyes
Were not in fault, for she was beautiful;
Mine ears, that heard her flattery; nor my heart,
That thought her like her seeming; it had been vicious
To have mistrusted her: yet, O my daughter!
That it was folly in me, thou mayst say,
And prove it in thy feeling. Heaven mend all!

Enter LUCIUS, IACHIMO, the SOOTHSAYER, and other Roman Prisoners, guarded; POSTHUMUS LEONATUS behind, and IMOGEN

Thou comest not, Caius, now for tribute that
The Britons have razed out, though with the loss
Of many a bold one; whose kinsmen have made suit
That their good souls may be appeased with slaughter
Of you their captives, which ourself have granted:
So think of your estate.

CAIUS LUCIUS
Consider, sir, the chance of war: the day
Was yours by accident; had it gone with us,

We should not, when the blood was cool, have threaten'd
Our prisoners with the sword. But since the gods
Will have it thus, that nothing but our lives
May be call'd ransom, let it come: sufficeth
A Roman with a Roman's heart can suffer:
Augustus lives to think on't: and so much
For my peculiar care. This one thing only
I will entreat; my boy, a Briton born,
Let him be ransom'd: never master had
A page so kind, so duteous, diligent,
So tender over his occasions, true,
So feat, so nurse-like: let his virtue join
With my request, which I make bold your highness
Cannot deny; he hath done no Briton harm,
Though he have served a Roman: save him, sir,
And spare no blood beside.

CYMBELINE
I have surely seen him:
His favour is familiar to me. Boy,
Thou hast look'd thyself into my grace,
And art mine own. I know not why, wherefore,
To say 'live, boy:' ne'er thank thy master; live:
And ask of Cymbeline what boon thou wilt,
Fitting my bounty and thy state, I'll give it;
Yea, though thou do demand a prisoner,
The noblest ta'en.

IMOGEN
I humbly thank your highness.

CAIUS LUCIUS
I do not bid thee beg my life, good lad;
And yet I know thou wilt.

IMOGEN
No, no: alack,
There's other work in hand: I see a thing
Bitter to me as death: your life, good master,
Must shuffle for itself.

CAIUS LUCIUS
The boy disdains me,
He leaves me, scorns me: briefly die their joys
That place them on the truth of girls and boys.
Why stands he so perplex'd?

CYMBELINE
What wouldst thou, boy?
I love thee more and more: think more and more

What's best to ask. Know'st him thou look'st on? speak,
Wilt have him live? Is he thy kin? thy friend?

IMOGEN
He is a Roman; no more kin to me
Than I to your highness; who, being born your vassal,
Am something nearer.

CYMBELINE
Wherefore eyest him so?

IMOGEN
I'll tell you, sir, in private, if you please
To give me hearing.

CYMBELINE
Ay, with all my heart,
And lend my best attention. What's thy name?

IMOGEN
Fidele, sir.

CYMBELINE
Thou'rt my good youth, my page;
I'll be thy master: walk with me; speak freely.

CYMBELINE and IMOGEN converse apart

BELARIUS
Is not this boy revived from death?

ARVIRAGUS
One sand another
Not more resembles that sweet rosy lad
Who died, and was Fidele. What think you?

GUIDERIUS
The same dead thing alive.

BELARIUS
Peace, peace! see further; he eyes us not; forbear;
Creatures may be alike: were 't he, I am sure
He would have spoke to us.

GUIDERIUS
But we saw him dead.

BELARIUS
Be silent; let's see further.

PISANIO

[Aside] It is my mistress:
Since she is living, let the time run on
To good or bad.

CYMBELINE and IMOGEN come forward

CYMBELINE
Come, stand thou by our side;
Make thy demand aloud.

To IACHIMO

Sir, step you forth;
Give answer to this boy, and do it freely;
Or, by our greatness and the grace of it,
Which is our honour, bitter torture shall
Winnow the truth from falsehood. On, speak to him.

IMOGEN
My boon is, that this gentleman may render
Of whom he had this ring.

POSTHUMUS LEONATUS
[Aside] What's that to him?

CYMBELINE
That diamond upon your finger, say
How came it yours?

IACHIMO
Thou'lt torture me to leave unspoken that
Which, to be spoke, would torture thee.

CYMBELINE
How! me?

IACHIMO
I am glad to be constrain'd to utter that
Which torments me to conceal. By villany
I got this ring: 'twas Leonatus' jewel;
Whom thou didst banish; and—which more may grieve thee,
As it doth me—a nobler sir ne'er lived
'Twixt sky and ground. Wilt thou hear more, my lord?

CYMBELINE
All that belongs to this.

IACHIMO
That paragon, thy daughter,—
For whom my heart drops blood, and my false spirits
Quail to remember—Give me leave; I faint.

CYMBELINE
My daughter! what of her? Renew thy strength:
I had rather thou shouldst live while nature will
Than die ere I hear more: strive, man, and speak.

IACHIMO
Upon a time,—unhappy was the clock
That struck the hour!—it was in Rome,—accursed
The mansion where!—'twas at a feast,—O, would
Our viands had been poison'd, or at least
Those which I heaved to head!—the good Posthumus—
What should I say? he was too good to be
Where ill men were; and was the best of all
Amongst the rarest of good ones,—sitting sadly,
Hearing us praise our loves of Italy
For beauty that made barren the swell'd boast
Of him that best could speak, for feature, laming
The shrine of Venus, or straight-pight Minerva,
Postures beyond brief nature, for condition,
A shop of all the qualities that man
Loves woman for, besides that hook of wiving,
Fairness which strikes the eye—

CYMBELINE
I stand on fire:
Come to the matter.

IACHIMO
All too soon I shall,
Unless thou wouldst grieve quickly. This Posthumus,
Most like a noble lord in love and one
That had a royal lover, took his hint;
And, not dispraising whom we praised,—therein
He was as calm as virtue—he began
His mistress' picture; which by his tongue being made,
And then a mind put in't, either our brags
Were crack'd of kitchen-trolls, or his description
Proved us unspeaking sots.

CYMBELINE
Nay, nay, to the purpose.

IACHIMO
Your daughter's chastity—there it begins.
He spake of her, as Dian had hot dreams,
And she alone were cold: whereat I, wretch,
Made scruple of his praise; and wager'd with him
Pieces of gold 'gainst this which then he wore
Upon his honour'd finger, to attain
In suit the place of's bed and win this ring

By hers and mine adultery. He, true knight,
No lesser of her honour confident
Than I did truly find her, stakes this ring;
And would so, had it been a carbuncle
Of Phoebus' wheel, and might so safely, had it
Been all the worth of's car. Away to Britain
Post I in this design: well may you, sir,
Remember me at court; where I was taught
Of your chaste daughter the wide difference
'Twixt amorous and villanous. Being thus quench'd
Of hope, not longing, mine Italian brain
'Gan in your duller Britain operate
Most vilely; for my vantage, excellent:
And, to be brief, my practise so prevail'd,
That I return'd with simular proof enough
To make the noble Leonatus mad,
By wounding his belief in her renown
With tokens thus, and thus; averting notes
Of chamber-hanging, pictures, this her bracelet,—
O cunning, how I got it!—nay, some marks
Of secret on her person, that he could not
But think her bond of chastity quite crack'd,
I having ta'en the forfeit. Whereupon—
Methinks, I see him now—

POSTHUMUS LEONATUS
[Advancing] Ay, so thou dost,
Italian fiend! Ay me, most credulous fool,
Egregious murderer, thief, any thing
That's due to all the villains past, in being,
To come! O, give me cord, or knife, or poison,
Some upright justicer! Thou, king, send out
For torturers ingenious: it is I
That all the abhorred things o' the earth amend
By being worse than they. I am Posthumus,
That kill'd thy daughter:—villain-like, I lie—
That caused a lesser villain than myself,
A sacrilegious thief, to do't: the temple
Of virtue was she; yea, and she herself.
Spit, and throw stone s, cast mire upon me, set
The dogs o' the street to bay me: every villain
Be call'd Posthumus Leonitus; and
Be villany less than 'twas! O Imogen!
My queen, my life, my wife! O Imogen,
Imogen, Imogen!

IMOGEN
Peace, my lord; hear, hear—

POSTHUMUS LEONATUS

Shall's have a play of this? Thou scornful page,
There lie thy part.

Striking her: she falls

PISANIO
O, gentlemen, help!
Mine and your mistress! O, my lord Posthumus!
You ne'er kill'd Imogen til now. Help, help!
Mine honour'd lady!

CYMBELINE
Does the world go round?

POSTHUMUS LEONATUS
How come these staggers on me?

PISANIO
Wake, my mistress!

CYMBELINE
If this be so, the gods do mean to strike me
To death with mortal joy.

PISANIO
How fares thy mistress?

IMOGEN
O, get thee from my sight;
Thou gavest me poison: dangerous fellow, hence!
Breathe not where princes are.

CYMBELINE
The tune of Imogen!

PISANIO
Lady,
The gods throw stones of sulphur on me, if
That box I gave you was not thought by me
A precious thing: I had it from the queen.

CYMBELINE
New matter still?

IMOGEN
It poison'd me.

CORNELIUS
O gods!
I left out one thing which the queen confess'd.
Which must approve thee honest: 'If Pisanio

Have,' said she, 'given his mistress that confection
Which I gave him for cordial, she is served
As I would serve a rat.'

CYMBELINE
What's this, Cornelius?

CORNELIUS
The queen, sir, very oft importuned me
To temper poisons for her, still pretending
The satisfaction of her knowledge only
In killing creatures vile, as cats and dogs,
Of no esteem: I, dreading that her purpose
Was of more danger, did compound for her
A certain stuff, which, being ta'en, would cease
The present power of life, but in short time
All offices of nature should again
Do their due functions. Have you ta'en of it?

IMOGEN
Most like I did, for I was dead.

BELARIUS
My boys,
There was our error.

GUIDERIUS
This is, sure, Fidele.

IMOGEN
Why did you throw your wedded lady from you?
Think that you are upon a rock; and now
Throw me again.

Embracing him

POSTHUMUS LEONATUS
Hang there like a fruit, my soul,
Till the tree die!

CYMBELINE
How now, my flesh, my child!
What, makest thou me a dullard in this act?
Wilt thou not speak to me?

IMOGEN
[Kneeling] Your blessing, sir.

BELARIUS

[To GUIDERIUS and ARVIRAGUS] Though you did love
this youth, I blame ye not:
You had a motive for't.

CYMBELINE
My tears that fall
Prove holy water on thee! Imogen,
Thy mother's dead.

IMOGEN
I am sorry for't, my lord.

CYMBELINE
O, she was nought; and long of her it was
That we meet here so strangely: but her son
Is gone, we know not how nor where.

PISANIO
My lord,
Now fear is from me, I'll speak troth. Lord Cloten,
Upon my lady's missing, came to me
With his sword drawn; foam'd at the mouth, and swore,
If I discover'd not which way she was gone,
It was my instant death. By accident,
had a feigned letter of my master's
Then in my pocket; which directed him
To seek her on the mountains near to Milford;
Where, in a frenzy, in my master's garments,
Which he enforced from me, away he posts
With unchaste purpose and with oath to violate
My lady's honour: what became of him
I further know not.

GUIDERIUS
Let me end the story:
I slew him there.

CYMBELINE
Marry, the gods forfend!
I would not thy good deeds should from my lips
Pluck a bard sentence: prithee, valiant youth,
Deny't again.

GUIDERIUS
I have spoke it, and I did it.

CYMBELINE
He was a prince.

GUIDERIUS

A most incivil one: the wrongs he did me
Were nothing prince-like; for he did provoke me
With language that would make me spurn the sea,
If it could so roar to me: I cut off's head;
And am right glad he is not standing here
To tell this tale of mine.

CYMBELINE
I am sorry for thee:
By thine own tongue thou art condemn'd, and must
Endure our law: thou'rt dead.

IMOGEN
That headless man
I thought had been my lord.

CYMBELINE
Bind the offender,
And take him from our presence.

BELARIUS
Stay, sir king:
This man is better than the man he slew,
As well descended as thyself; and hath
More of thee merited than a band of Clotens
Had ever scar for.

To the GUARD

Let his arms alone;
They were not born for bondage.

CYMBELINE
Why, old soldier,
Wilt thou undo the worth thou art unpaid for,
By tasting of our wrath? How of descent
As good as we?

ARVIRAGUS
In that he spake too far.

CYMBELINE
And thou shalt die for't.

BELARIUS
We will die all three:
But I will prove that two on's are as good
As I have given out him. My sons, I must,
For mine own part, unfold a dangerous speech,
Though, haply, well for you.

ARVIRAGUS
Your danger's ours.

GUIDERIUS
And our good his.

BELARIUS
Have at it then, by leave.
Thou hadst, great king, a subject who
Was call'd Belarius.

CYMBELINE
What of him? he is
A banish'd traitor.

BELARIUS
He it is that hath
Assumed this age; indeed a banish'd man;
I know not how a traitor.

CYMBELINE
Take him hence:
The whole world shall not save him.

BELARIUS
Not too hot:
First pay me for the nursing of thy sons;
And let it be confiscate all, so soon
As I have received it.

CYMBELINE
Nursing of my sons!

BELARIUS
I am too blunt and saucy: here's my knee:
Ere I arise, I will prefer my sons;
Then spare not the old father. Mighty sir,
These two young gentlemen, that call me father
And think they are my sons, are none of mine;
They are the issue of your loins, my liege,
And blood of your begetting.

CYMBELINE
How! my issue!

BELARIUS
So sure as you your father's. I, old Morgan,
Am that Belarius whom you sometime banish'd:
Your pleasure was my mere offence, my punishment
Itself, and all my treason; that I suffer'd
Was all the harm I did. These gentle princes—

For such and so they are—these twenty years
Have I train'd up: those arts they have as I
Could put into them; my breeding was, sir, as
Your highness knows. Their nurse, Euriphile,
Whom for the theft I wedded, stole these children
Upon my banishment: I moved her to't,
Having received the punishment before,
For that which I did then: beaten for loyalty
Excited me to treason: their dear loss,
The more of you 'twas felt, the more it shaped
Unto my end of stealing them. But, gracious sir,
Here are your sons again; and I must lose
Two of the sweet'st companions in the world.
The benediction of these covering heavens
Fall on their heads like dew! for they are worthy
To inlay heaven with stars.

CYMBELINE
Thou weep'st, and speak'st.
The service that you three have done is more
Unlike than this thou tell'st. I lost my children:
If these be they, I know not how to wish
A pair of worthier sons.

BELARIUS
Be pleased awhile.
This gentleman, whom I call Polydore,
Most worthy prince, as yours, is true Guiderius:
This gentleman, my Cadwal, Arviragus,
Your younger princely son; he, sir, was lapp'd
In a most curious mantle, wrought by the hand
Of his queen mother, which for more probation
I can with ease produce.

CYMBELINE
Guiderius had
Upon his neck a mole, a sanguine star;
It was a mark of wonder.

BELARIUS
This is he;
Who hath upon him still that natural stamp:
It was wise nature's end in the donation,
To be his evidence now.

CYMBELINE
O, what, am I
A mother to the birth of three? Ne'er mother
Rejoiced deliverance more. Blest pray you be,
That, after this strange starting from your orbs,

may reign in them now! O Imogen,
Thou hast lost by this a kingdom.

IMOGEN
No, my lord;
I have got two worlds by 't. O my gentle brothers,
Have we thus met? O, never say hereafter
But I am truest speaker you call'd me brother,
When I was but your sister; I you brothers,
When ye were so indeed.

CYMBELINE
Did you e'er meet?

ARVIRAGUS
Ay, my good lord.

GUIDERIUS
And at first meeting loved;
Continued so, until we thought he died.

CORNELIUS
By the queen's dram she swallow'd.

CYMBELINE
O rare instinct!
When shall I hear all through? This fierce abridgement
Hath to it circumstantial branches, which
Distinction should be rich in. Where? how lived You?
And when came you to serve our Roman captive?
How parted with your brothers? how first met them?
Why fled you from the court? and whither? These,
And your three motives to the battle, with
I know not how much more, should be demanded;
And all the other by-dependencies,
From chance to chance: but nor the time nor place
Will serve our long inter'gatories. See,
Posthumus anchors upon Imogen,
And she, like harmless lightning, throws her eye
On him, her brother, me, her master, hitting
Each object with a joy: the counterchange
Is severally in all. Let's quit this ground,
And smoke the temple with our sacrifices.

To BELARIUS

Thou art my brother; so we'll hold thee ever.

IMOGEN
You are my father too, and did relieve me,
To see this gracious season.

CYMBELINE
All o'erjoy'd,
Save these in bonds: let them be joyful too,
For they shall taste our comfort.

IMOGEN
My good master,
I will yet do you service.

CAIUS LUCIUS
Happy be you!

CYMBELINE
The forlorn soldier, that so nobly fought,
He would have well becomed this place, and graced
The thankings of a king.

POSTHUMUS LEONATUS
I am, sir,
The soldier that did company these three
In poor beseeming; 'twas a fitment for
The purpose I then follow'd. That I was he,
Speak, Iachimo: I had you down and might
Have made you finish.

IACHIMO
[Kneeling] I am down again:
But now my heavy conscience sinks my knee,
As then your force did. Take that life, beseech you,
Which I so often owe: but your ring first;
And here the bracelet of the truest princess
That ever swore her faith.

POSTHUMUS LEONATUS
Kneel not to me:
The power that I have on you is, to spare you;
The malice towards you to forgive you: live,
And deal with others better.

CYMBELINE
Nobly doom'd!
We'll learn our freeness of a son-in-law;
Pardon's the word to all.

ARVIRAGUS
You holp us, sir,
As you did mean indeed to be our brother;
Joy'd are we that you are.

POSTHUMUS LEONATUS

Your servant, princes. Good my lord of Rome,
Call forth your soothsayer: as I slept, methought
Great Jupiter, upon his eagle back'd,
Appear'd to me, with other spritely shows
Of mine own kindred: when I waked, I found
This label on my bosom; whose containing
Is so from sense in hardness, that I can
Make no collection of it: let him show
His skill in the construction.

CAIUS LUCIUS
Philarmonus!

Soothsayer
Here, my good lord.

CAIUS LUCIUS
Read, and declare the meaning.

Soothsayer
[Reads] 'When as a lion's whelp shall, to himself unknown, without seeking find, and be embraced by a piece of tender air; and when from a stately cedar shall be lopped branches, which, being dead many years, shall after revive, be jointed to the old stock, and freshly grow; then shall Posthumus end his miseries, Britain be fortunate and flourish in peace and plenty.'
Thou, Leonatus, art the lion's whelp;
The fit and apt construction of thy name,
Being Leonatus, doth import so much.

To CYMBELINE

The piece of tender air, thy virtuous daughter,
Which we call 'mollis aer;' and 'mollis aer'
We term it 'mulier:' which 'mulier' I divine
Is this most constant wife; who, even now,
Answering the letter of the oracle,
Unknown to you, unsought, were clipp'd about
With this most tender air.

CYMBELINE
This hath some seeming.

Soothsayer
The lofty cedar, royal Cymbeline,
Personates thee: and thy lopp'd branches point
Thy two sons forth; who, by Belarius stol'n,
For many years thought dead, are now revived,
To the majestic cedar join'd, whose issue
Promises Britain peace and plenty.

CYMBELINE

Well
My peace we will begin. And, Caius Lucius,
Although the victor, we submit to Caesar,
And to the Roman empire; promising
To pay our wonted tribute, from the which
We were dissuaded by our wicked queen;
Whom heavens, in justice, both on her and hers,
Have laid most heavy hand.

Soothsayer
The fingers of the powers above do tune
The harmony of this peace. The vision
Which I made known to Lucius, ere the stroke
Of this yet scarce-cold battle, at this instant
Is full accomplish'd; for the Roman eagle,
From south to west on wing soaring aloft,
Lessen'd herself, and in the beams o' the sun
So vanish'd: which foreshow'd our princely eagle,
The imperial Caesar, should again unite
His favour with the radiant Cymbeline,
Which shines here in the west.

CYMBELINE
Laud we the gods;
And let our crooked smokes climb to their nostrils
From our blest altars. Publish we this peace
To all our subjects. Set we forward: let
A Roman and a British ensign wave
Friendly together: so through Lud's-town march:
And in the temple of great Jupiter
Our peace we'll ratify; seal it with feasts.
Set on there! Never was a war did cease,
Ere bloody hands were wash'd, with such a peace.

Exeunt

William Shakespeare – A Short Biography

The life of William Shakespeare, arguably the most significant figure in the Western literary canon, is relatively unknown. Even the exact date of his birth is uncertain. April 23rd, the date now generally accepted to be the date of his birth, is a result of a scholarly mistake and the appealing coincidence of its being also the day of his death.

That so little is known about a writer with such great literary scope and accomplishment has naturally invited speculation and conspiracy theories about the authenticity of his authorship, his influence and even his existence.

Shakespeare was born in Stratford-upon-Avon in 1565, possibly on the 23rd April, St. George's Day, and baptised there on 26th April. His father was John Shakespeare, a successful glover and alderman who hailed from Snitterfield. His mother was Mary Arden, whose father was an affluent landowner. In total their union bore eight children; William was the third of these and the eldest surviving son.

Although there is no hard evidence on his education it is widely agreed among scholars that William attended the King's New School in Stratford which was chartered as a free school in 1553. This school was only a quarter of a mile from the house in which he spent his childhood, but since there are no attendance records existing it is assumed, rather than known, this was the base for his education.

Although the quality of education in a grammar school at that time varied wildly the curriculum did not, a key aspect of which, by royal decree, was Latin, and it is undoubtable that the school will have delivered an intensive education in Latin grammar, drawing heavily on the work of the classical Latin authors. If Shakespeare did attend this school then it is very likely the starting point for the fascination with and extensive knowledge of the classical Latin authors which would inform and inspire so much of his work began.

Little more detail is known of William's childhood, or his early teenage years, until, at the age of 18, he married Anne Hathaway, who was 26 and from the nearby village of Shottery. Her father was a yeoman farmer, and their family home a small farmhouse in the village. In his will he left her £6 13s 4d, six pounds, thirteen shillings and fourpence, to be paid on her wedding day. On November 27th, 1582 the consistory court of the Diocese of Worcester issued a marriage licence, and on the 28th two of Hathaway's neighbours, Fulk Sandells and John Richardson, posted bonds which guaranteed that there were no lawful claims to impede the marriage along with a surety of £40 to act as a financial guarantee for the wedding.

The marriage was conducted in some haste since, unusually, the marriage banns were read only once instead of the more normal three times, a decision which would have been taken by the Worcester chancellor. This haste is no doubt due to the child Anne delivered their first child, Susanna, six months later. Susanna, was baptised on May 26th, 1583. Several scholars have voiced their opinion that the wedding was imposed on a reluctant Shakespeare by Hathaway's outraged parents, although, again, there is nothing to formally support the theory. It has been further argued that the circumstances surrounding the wedding, particularly those of the neighbourly assurances, indicate that Shakespeare was involved with two women at the time of his marriage. According to the theory proposed by the early twentieth century scholar Frank Harris, Shakespeare had already chosen to marry a woman named Anne Whateley. It was only once this proposed union became known that Hathaway's outraged family forced him to marry their daughter. Harris goes on to surmise that Shakespeare considered the affair entrapment, and that this led to his wholesale despising of her, a "loathing for his wife [which] was measureless" and which ultimately caused him to leave Stratford and her and make for the theatre. But equally other scholars such as John Aubrey have responded to this with evidence that Shakespeare returned to Stratford every year which, if true, would rather diminish Harris's claim that Hathaway had poisoned Stratford for Shakespeare.

Harris's theory aside, Shakespeare and Hathaway had two more children, twins Hamnet and Judith, baptised on February 2nd,1585. Hamnet, Shakespeare's only son, died during one of the frequent outbreaks of bubonic plague and was buried on the August 11th, 1596, at the age of only eleven.

Little is known of Shakespeare's life during the years following the birth of the twins until he appears mentioned in relation to the London theatres in 1592, apart from a fleeting mention in the complaints bill of a legal case which came before the Queen's Bench court at Westminster, dated Michaelmas Term 1588 and October 9th, 1589. Despite this period of time being referred to in scholarly circles as Shakespeare's "lost years", there are several stories, apocryphal in nature, which are attributed to Shakespeare. For example, there is a legend in Stratford that he fled the town in order to avoid prosecution for poaching deer on the estate of Thomas Lucy, a local squire. It is also supposed that Shakespeare went so far as to take revenge on Lucy, a politician whose Protestantism opposed Shakespeare's Catholic childhood, by writing the following lampooning ballad about him:

> A parliament member, a justice of peace,
> At home a poor scarecrow, at London an ass,
> If lousy is Lucy as some folks miscall it
> Then Lucy is lousy whatever befall it.

However amusing the ballad and legend may be in imagining the life of a young Shakespeare, youthfully mischievous and still developing the wit, sense of adventure and humour which would become integral aspects of his writing, there is simply no evidence either to support the theory or to suggest that Shakespeare penned the ballad. Alongside this are suggestions that he began his theatrical career while minding the horses of the patrons of the London theatres and that he spent some time as a schoolmaster employed by one Alexander Hoghton, a Catholic landowner in Lancashire, in whose will is named "William Shakeshafte". However, this was a popular name in the Lancashire area at that time and there is no evidence that this referred to Shakespeare. The wealth of his writing makes it a frustrating exercise to learn more of his life and the manner in which he achieved those outstanding and lionized works.

Interestingly, the reference to Shakespeare in 1592 which ends the "lost years" is a piece of theatrical criticism by playwright Robert Greene in *Groats-Worth of Wit*. In a scathing passage Greene writes "…there is an upstart Crow, beautified with our feathers, that with his *Tiger's heart wrapped in a Player's hide*, supposes he is as well able to bombast out a blank verse as the best of you: and being an absolute *Johannes factotum*, is in his own conceit the only Shake-scene in a country." From this entry we can make some important inferences which shed light on Shakespeare's career, the first of which is that to be acknowledged, even negatively, by a playwright such as Robert Greene, by this point he must have been making significant impact on the London stage as a writer. Also of significance is the very meaning of the words themselves, for it is generally acknowledged that Shakespeare is being accused of writing with a lofty ambition beyond his capabilities and, more importantly, the capabilities of his contemporaries who were educated at Oxford and Cambridge. Within this remark, then, is an inherent snobbery which Shakespeare would come to resent and ultimately challenge in his writing. Though Greene's parody of "Oh, tiger's heart wrapped in a woman's hide" makes reference to *Henry VI, Part 3*, it is likely that Greene's opinion of Shakespeare was in part informed by another of Shakespeare's plays which was heavily criticised, *Titus Adronicus*, believed to have been written between 1588 and 1593. It was his first attempt at tragedy, almost prototypical, and was written at a time when, according to the scholar Jonathan Bate, he was "experimenting with ways of writing about and representing rape and seduction". Drawing heavily on the sixth book of Ovid's *Metamorphoses* as its main source of inspiration for the rape and mutilation of Lavinia, it offended the sensibilities of the more highbrow members of its audience, whilst presumably also simultaneously intimidating them with its detailed knowledge of Ovid, a writer typically considered the reserve of the university-educated. Not only, then, was Shakespeare demonstrating a knowledge of classical literature which they thought befitted only a traditional scholar and thereby shining a light to the snobbery and exclusivity of such an education, but he was doing it radically and brilliantly.

By 1594 the Lord Chamberlain's Men had recognised his worthiness as a playwright and were performing his works. With the advantage of Shakespeare's progressive writing they rapidly became London's leading company of players, affording him more exposure and, following the death of

Queen Elizabeth in 1603, a royal patent by the new king, James I, at which point they changed their name to the King's Men.

Before this success, though, several company members had formed a partnership to build their own theatre which came to be on the south bank of the river Thames, the now-famous and reconstructed Globe theatre. Though it is unclear precisely what Shakespeare's involvement in this venture was, records of his property and investments indicate that he came to be rich during this period, buying the second-largest house in Stratford, called New Place, in 1597, which he made his family home. Prior to this he was living in the parish of St Helen's Bishopsgate, north of the River Thames. He continued to spend most of his time at work in London and from about 1598-1602, he seems to have lived in the Paris Gardens area of Bankside south of the river near The Globe.

Despite efforts to pirate his work, Shakespeare's name was by 1598 so well known that it had already become a selling point in its own right on title pages.

An interesting aside is that theatres were mostly constructed on the south bank of the Thames (then part of the county of Surrey) as performing in London itself was thought to be a bad influence on the masses and subject to periodic bouts of censorship, repression and closing of venues which in the City itself was mainly courtyards and open areas at the many Inns.

Excluded from the City purpose built theatres began to be constructed outside the City limits. This area of the Thames though was rough and naturally vibrant with all sorts of characters, many of them of dubious nature or even criminal. It was also prone, due to its over-crowding and bad sanitation, to bouts of bubonic plague and other diseases particularly during the summer which was a further reason for the theatres there being closed. The Curtain, The Rose, The Swan, The Fortune, The Blackfriars and of course The Globe were all purpose built and situated here, some with an audience capacity approaching 3,000.

The first known printed copies of Shakespeare's plays date from 1594 in quarto editions, though these quarto editions are often considered "bad", a term referring to the likelihood of specific quarto editions being based on, for example, a reconstruction of a play as it was witnessed, rather than Shakespeare's original manuscript. The best example of such memorial reconstruction can be found in the differences between the first and second quarto editions of *Hamlet*. In examining Hamlet's most famous soliloquy, "to be or not to be", we can immediately recognise significant differences. First, the familiar second quarto version:

> To be, or not to be; that is the question:
> Whether 'tis nobler in the mind to suffer
> The slings and arrows of outrageous fortune,
> Or to take arms against a sea of troubles,
> And, by opposing, end them.

And, by contrast, the first quarto version:

> To be, or not to be, I there's the point,
> To Die, to sleep, is that all? I all:

For scholar Henry David Gray the first quarto lines are emblematic of "a distorted version of the completed drama filled out and revised by an inferior poet" and based, he goes on to argue, on the fractured memories of the play as witnessed and performed by the actor playing Marcellus. Gray, and several other critics, consider the first quarto a pirated copy, printed in haste without the writer's permission in an attempt to make quick money following the success of the play in the theatre. In understanding the significance of Marcellus to the theory it is imperative to note that the authenticity of each quarto is based on its similarities to the version of the play found in the first folio, printed in 1623 and believed to be authorised by Shakespeare. Therefore, since in the folio version of *Hamlet* the "to be or not to be" soliloquy is virtually identical to that of the second quarto, it is believed that the second was authored by Shakespeare himself and that the first, by its considerable differences, must therefore be in some way compromised. However, when read in comparison to the folio version, the only character whose lines are almost entirely perfect are those spoken by Marcellus, which, since dramatic practice at the time was for actors to be given only their own lines and three or four word 'cues' based on the lines preceding theirs, suggests that the first quarto is a memorial reconstruction of the play written by the actor who played Marcellus. Having committed his own lines to memory he was able to reproduce them accurately, but was left to fill in the remaining lines and plot from memory which accounts for the truncated and often vastly inferior writing in the first quarto.

According to the remaining cast lists from the period, Shakespeare remained an actor throughout his career as a writer, and it is thought he continued to act after he retired his pen. In 1616 he is recorded in the cast list in Ben Jonson's collected *Works* in the plays *Man in His Humour* 1598) and *Sejanus His Fall* (1603), though some scholars consider his absence from the list of Jonson's *Volpone* evidence that, by 1605, his acting career was nearing its end. Despite this in the First Folio he is listed as one of "the Principle Actors in all these Plays", several of which were only staged after *Volpone*.

By 1604 he had moved again, remaining north of the river, to an area near St. Paul's Cathedral where he rented a fine room amongst fine houses from Christopher Mountjoy, a French hatmaker and Huguenot.

The Anglo-Welsh poet John Davies of Hereford wrote in 1610 that "good Will" tended to play "kingly" roles, suggesting he was still on stage, perhaps now performing the more mature kings such as Lear and Henry VI. There has even been the suggestion that Shakespeare played the ghost of Hamlet's father, though there is little evidence to suggest it.

In 1608 the King's Men purchased the Blackfriars theatre from Henry Evans, and according to Cuthbert Burbage, one of the most highly regarded actors of the time, "placed many players" there "which were Heminges, Condell, Shakespeare, etc." A 1609 lawsuit brought against John Addenbrooke in Stratford on the 7th of June describes Shakespeare as "generosus nuper in curia domini Jacobi" (a gentleman recently at the court of King James) which indicates that by this time he was spending more time in Stratford. A likely cause of this was the bubonic plague, frequent outbreaks of which demanded the equally frequent closing of places of public gathering, principle among which were the theatres. Between May 1603 and February 1610 the theatres were closed for a total of 60 months, meaning there was no acting work and nobody to perform new plays. Though in 1610 Shakespeare returned to Stratford and it is supposed lived with his wife, he made frequent visits to London between 1611-14, being called as a witness in the trial *Bellott v. Mountjoy*, a case addressing concerns about the marriage settlement of Mountjoy's daughter, Mary. In March 1613 he purchased a gatehouse in the former Blackfriars priory, and spent several weeks in the city with his son-in-law John Hall, a physician, married to his daughter Susanna, from November 1614.

No plays are attributed to Shakespeare after 1613, and the last few plays he wrote before this time were in collaboration with other writers, one of whom is likely to be John Fletcher who succeeded him as the house playwright for the King's Men.

In early 1616 his daughter Judith married Thomas Quiney, a vintner and tobacconist. He signed his last will and testament on March 25th, of the same year, and the following day Quiney was ordered to do public penance for having fathered an illegitimate child with a woman named Margaret Wheeler who had died during childbirth which had enabled Quiney to cover up the scandal. This public humiliation would have been embarrassing for Shakespeare and his family.

William Shakespeare died two months later on April 23rd, 1616, survived by his wife and two daughters.

According to his will the bulk of his considerable estate was left to his elder daughter Susanna, with the instruction that she pass it down intact to "the first son of her body". However, though Susanna and Judith had four children between them they all died without progeny, ending Shakespeare's direct lineage. Also in his will was the instruction that his "second best bed" be left to his wife Anne, likely an insult, though the bed was possibly matrimonial and therefore of significant sentimental value.

He was buried two days after his death in the chancel of the Holy Trinity Church in Stratford-Upon-Avon.

The epitaph on the slab which covers his grave includes the following passage,

> Good frend for Iesvs sake forbeare,
> To digg the dvst encloased heare.
> Bleste be ye man yt spares thes stones,
> And cvrst be he yt moves my bones

which, in modern translation, reads

> Good friend, for Jesus's sake forbear,
> To dig the dust enclosed here.
> Blessed be the man that spares these stones,
> And cursed be he that moves my bones.

At some point before 1623 there was a funerary monument erected in his memory on the north wall of Stratford-upon-Avon which features a half-effigy of him writing, and which likens him to Nestor, Socrates and Virgil.

On January 29th, 1741 a white marble memorial statue to him was erected in Poets' Corner in Westminster Abbey.

Though there have been many monuments built around the world in memory of Shakespeare, undoubtedly the greatest memorial of all is the body of work which became the foundation of Western literary canon and an inspiration for every generation.

William Shakespeare – A Concise Bibliography

| 1589 | Comedy of Errors (Comedy) |
| 1590 | Henry VI, Part II (History) |

	Henry VI, Part III (History)
1591	Henry VI, Part I (History)
1592	Richard III (History)
1593	Taming of the Shrew (Comedy) Titus Andronicus (Tragedy) Venus and Adonis (Poem)
1594	Rape of Lucrece (Poem) Romeo and Juliet (Tragedy) Two Gentlemen of Verona (Comedy) Love's Labour's Lost (Comedy)
1595	Richard II (History) Midsummer Night's Dream (Comedy)
1596	King John (History) Merchant of Venice (Comedy)
1597	Henry IV, Part I (History) Henry IV, Part II (History)
1598	Passionate Pilgrim (Poem) Henry V (History) Much Ado about Nothing (Comedy)
1599	Twelfth Night (Comedy) As You Like It (Comedy) Julius Caesar (Tragedy)
1600	Hamlet (Tragedy) Merry Wives of Windsor (Comedy)
1601	Troilus and Cressida (Comedy)
1601	Phoenix and the Turtle (Poem))
1602	All's Well That Ends Well (Comedy)
1604	Othello (Tragedy) Measure for Measure
1605	King Lear (Tragedy) Macbeth (Tragedy)
1606	Antony and Cleopatra (Tragedy)
1607	Coriolanus (Tragedy) Timon of Athens (Tragedy)

1608	Pericles (Comedy)	
1609	Cymbeline (Comedy)	
	Lover's Complaint (Poem)	
1610	Winter's Tale (Comedy)	
1611	Tempest (Comedy)	
1612	Henry VIII (History)	

As regards his 154 sonnets it is almost impossible to date each individually though collectively they were first published in 1609, with two having been published in 1599.

Shakspeare; or, the Poet by Ralph Waldo Emerson

Great (1) men are more distinguished by range and extent than by originality. If we require the originality which consists in weaving, like a spider, their web from their own bowels; in finding clay and making bricks and building the house; no great men are original. Nor does valuable originality consist in unlikeness to other men. The hero is in the press of knights and the thick of events; and seeing what men want and sharing their desire, he adds the needful length of sight and of arm, to come at the desired point. The greatest genius is the most indebted man. A poet is no rattle-brain, saying what comes uppermost, and, because he says every thing, saying at last something good; but a heart in unison with his time and country. There is nothing whimsical and fantastic in his production, but sweet and sad earnest, freighted with the weightiest convictions and pointed with the most determined aim which any man or class knows of in his times. (2)

The Genius of our life is jealous of individuals, and will not have any individual great, except through the general. There is no choice to genius. A great man does not wake up on some fine morning and say, 'I am full of life, I will go to sea and find an Antarctic continent: to-day I will square the circle: I will ransack botany and find a new food for man: I have a new architecture in my mind: I foresee a new mechanic power:' no, but he finds himself in the river of the thoughts and events, forced onward by the ideas and necessities of his contemporaries. (3) He stands where all the eyes of men look one way, and their hands all point in the direction in which he should go. The Church has reared him amidst rites and pomps, and he carries out the advice which her music gave him, and builds a cathedral needed by her chants and processions. He finds a war raging: it educates him, by trumpet, in barracks, and he betters the instruction. He finds two counties groping to bring coal, or flour, or fish, from the place of production to the place of consumption, and he hits on a railroad. Every master has found his materials collected, and his power lay in his sympathy with his people and in his love of the materials he wrought in. What an economy of power! and what a compensation for the shortness of life! All is done to his hand. The world has brought him thus far on his way. The human race has gone out before him, sunk the hills, filled the hollows and bridged the rivers. Men, nations, poets, artisans, women, all have worked for him, and he enters into their labors. Choose any other thing, out of the line of tendency, out of the national feeling and history, and he would have all to do for himself: his powers would be expended in the first preparations. Great genial power, one would almost say, consists in not being original at all; in being altogether receptive; in letting the world do all, and suffering the spirit of the hour to pass unobstructed through the mind. (4)

Shakspeare's youth fell in a time when the English people were importunate for dramatic entertainments. The court took offence easily at political allusions and attempted to suppress them. The Puritans, a growing and energetic party, and the religious among the Anglican church, would suppress them. But the people wanted them. Inn-yards, houses without roofs, and extemporaneous enclosures at country fairs were the ready theatres of strolling players. The people had tasted this new joy; and, as we could not hope to suppress newspapers now,—no, not by the strongest party,— neither then could king, prelate, or puritan, alone or united, suppress an organ which was ballad, epic, newspaper, caucus, lecture, Punch and library, at the same time. Probably king, prelate and puritan, all found their own account in it. It had become, by all causes, a national interest,—by no means conspicuous, so that some great scholar would have thought of treating it in an English history,—but not a whit less considerable because it was cheap and of no account, like a baker's-shop. The best proof of its vitality is the crowd of writers which suddenly broke into this field; Kyd, Marlow, Greene, Jonson, Chapman, Dekker, Webster, Heywood, Middleton, Peele, Ford, Massinger, Beaumont and Fletcher.

The secure possession, by the stage, of the public mind, is of the first importance to the poet who works for it. (5) He loses no time in idle experiments. Here is audience and expectation prepared. In the case of Shakspeare there is much more. At the time when he left Stratford and went up to London, a great body of stage-plays of all dates and writers existed in manuscript and were in turn produced on the boards. Here is the Tale of Troy, which the audience will bear hearing some part of, every week; the Death of Julius Cæsar, and other stories out of Plutarch, which they never tire of; a shelf full of English history, from the chronicles of Brut and Arthur, down to the royal Henries, which men hear eagerly; and a string of doleful tragedies, merry Italian tales and Spanish voyages, which all the London 'prentices know. All the mass has been treated, with more or less skill, by every playwright, and the prompter has the soiled and tattered manuscripts. It is now no longer possible to say who wrote them first. They have been the property of the Theatre so long, and so many rising geniuses have enlarged or altered them, inserting a speech or a whole scene, or adding a song, that no man can any longer claim copyright in this work of numbers. Happily, no man wishes to. They are not yet desired in that way. We have few readers, many spectators and hearers. They had best lie where they are.

Shakspeare, in common with his comrades, esteemed the mass of old plays waste stock, in which any experiment could be freely tried. Had the prestige which hedges about a modern tragedy existed, nothing could have been done. The rude warm blood of the living England circulated in the play, as in street-ballads, and gave body which he wanted to his airy and majestic fancy. The poet needs a ground in popular tradition on which he may work, and which, again, may restrain his art within the due temperance. It holds him to the people, supplies a foundation for his edifice, and in furnishing so much work done to his hand, leaves him at leisure and in full strength for the audacities of his imagination. In short, the poet owes to his legend what sculpture owed to the temple. Sculpture in Egypt and in Greece grew up in subordination to architecture. It was the ornament of the temple wall: at first a rude relief carved on pediments, then the relief became bolder and a head or arm was projected from the wall; the groups being still arranged with reference to the building, which serves also as a frame to hold the figures; and when at last the greatest freedom of style and treatment was reached, the prevailing genius of architecture still enforced a certain calmness and continence in the statue. As soon as the statue was begun for itself, and with no reference to the temple or palace, the art began to decline: freak, extravagance and exhibition took the place of the old temperance. This balance-wheel, which the sculptor found in architecture, the perilous irritability of poetic talent found in the accumulated dramatic materials to which the people were already wonted, and which had a certain excellence which no single genius, however extraordinary, could hope to create.

In point of fact it appears that Shakspeare did owe debts in all directions, and was able to use whatever he found; and the amount of indebtedness may be inferred from Malone's laborious computations in regard to the First, Second and Third parts of Henry VI., in which, "out of 6043 lines, 1771 were written by some author preceding Shakspeare, 2373 by him, on the foundation laid by him by his predecessors, and 1899 were entirely his own." And the proceeding investigation hardly leaves a single drama of his absolute invention. Malone's sentence is an important piece of external history. In Henry VIII. I think I see plainly the cropping out of the original rock on which his own finer stratum was laid. The first play was written by a superior, thoughtful man, with a vicious ear. I can mark his lines, and know well their cadence. See Wolsey's soliloquy, and the following scene with Cromwell, where instead of the metre of Shakspeare, whose secret is that the thought constructs the tune, so that reading for the sense will best bring out the rhythm,—here the lines are constructed on a given tune, and the verse has even a trace of pulpit eloquence. But the play contains through all its length unmistakable traits of Shakspeare's hand, and some passages, as the account of the coronation, are like autographs. What is odd, the compliment to Queen Elizabeth is in the bad rhythm. (6)

Shakspeare knew that tradition supplies a better fable than any invention can. If he lost any credit of design, he augmented his resources; and, at that day, our petulant demand for originality was not so much pressed. There was no literature for the million. The universal reading, the cheap press, were unknown. A great poet who appears in illiterate times, absorbs into his sphere all the light which is any where radiating. Every intellectual jewel, every flower of sentiment it is his fine office to bring to his people; and he comes to value his memory equally with his invention. (7) He is therefore little solicitous whence his thoughts have been derived; whether through translation, whether through tradition, whether by travel in distant countries, whether by inspiration; from whatever source, they are equally welcome to his uncritical audience. Nay, he borrows very near home. Other men say wise things as well as he; only they say a good many foolish things, and do not know when they have spoken wisely. He knows the sparkle of the true stone, and puts it in high place, wherever he finds it. (8) Such is the happy position of Homer perhaps; of Chaucer, of Saadi. They felt that all wit was their wit. And they are librarians and historiographers, as well as poets. Each romancer was heir and dispenser of all the hundred tales of the world,—

"Presenting Thebes' and Pelops' line
And the tale of Troy divine." (9)

The influence of Chaucer is conspicuous in all our early literature; and more recently not only Pope and Dryden have been beholden to him, but, in the whole society of English writers, a large unacknowledged debt is easily traced. One is charmed with the opulence which feeds so many pensioners. But Chaucer is a huge borrower. Chaucer, it seems, drew continually, through Lydgate and Caxton, from Guido di Colonna, whose Latin romance of the Trojan war was in turn a compilation from Dares Phrygius, Ovid and Statius. Then Petrarch, Boccaccio and the Provençal poets are his benefactors: the Romaunt of the Rose is only judicious translation from William of Lorris and John of Meung: Troilus and Creseide, from Lollius of Urbino: The Cock and the Fox, from the Lais of Marie: The House of Fame, from the French or Italian: and poor Gower he uses as if he were only a brick-kiln or stone-quarry out of which to build his house. (10) He steals by this apology,—that what he takes has no worth where he finds it and the greatest where he leaves it. It has come to be practically a sort of rule in literature, that a man having once shown himself capable of original writing, is entitled thenceforth to steal from the writings of others at discretion. Thought is the property of him who can entertain it and of him who can adequately place it. A certain awkwardness marks the use of borrowed thoughts; but as soon as we have learned what to do with them they become our own.

Thus all originality is relative. Every thinker is retrospective. The learned member of the legislature, at Westminster or at Washington, speaks and votes for thousands. Show us the constituency, and the now invisible channels by which the senator is made aware of their wishes; the crowd of practical and knowing men, who, by correspondence or conversation, are feeding him with evidence, anecdotes and estimates, and it will bereave his fine attitude and resistance of something of their impressiveness. As Sir Robert Peel and Mr. Webster vote, so Locke and Rousseau think, for thousands; and so there were fountains all around Homer, (11) Menu, Saadi, or Milton, from which they drew; friends, lovers, books, traditions, proverbs,—all perished—which, if seen, would go to reduce the wonder. Did the bard speak with authority? Did he feel himself overmatched by any companion? The appeal is to the consciousness of the writer. Is there at last in his breast a Delphi whereof to ask concerning any thought or thing, whether it be verily so, yea or nay? and to have answer, and to rely on that? All the debts which such a man could contract to other wit would never disturb his consciousness of originality; for the ministrations of books and of other minds are a whiff of smoke to that most private reality with which he has conversed. (12)

It is easy to see that what is best written or done by genius in the world, was no man's work, but came by wide social labor, when a thousand wrought like one, sharing the same impulse. Our English Bible is a wonderful specimen of the strength and music of the English language. But it was not made by one man, or at one time; but centuries and churches brought it to perfection. There never was a time when there was not some translation existing. The Liturgy, admired for its energy and pathos, is an anthology of the piety of ages and nations, a translation of the prayers and forms of the Catholic church,—these collected, too, in long periods, from the prayers and meditations of every saint and sacred writer all over the world. (13) Grotius makes the like remark in respect to the Lord's Prayer, that the single clauses of which it is composed were already in use in the time of Christ, in the Rabbinical forms. He picked out the grains of gold. The nervous language of the Common Law, the impressive forms of our courts and the precision and substantial truth of the legal distinctions, are the contribution of all the sharp-sighted, strong-minded men who have lived in the countries where these laws govern. The translation of Plutarch gets its excellence by being translation on translation. There never was a time when there was none. All the truly idiomatic and national phrases are kept, and all others successively picked out and thrown away. Something like the same process had gone on, long before, with the originals of these books. The world takes liberties with world-books. Vedas, Æsop's Fables, Pilpay, Arabian Nights, Cid, Iliad, Robin Hood, Scottish Minstrelsy, are not the work of single men. In the composition of such works the time thinks, the market thinks, the mason, the carpenter, the merchant, the farmer, the fop, all think for us. Every book supplies its time with one good word; every municipal law, every trade, every folly of the day; and the generic catholic genius who is not afraid or ashamed to owe his originality to the originality of all, stands with the next age as the recorder and embodiment of his own. (14)

We have to thank the researches of antiquaries, and the Shakspeare Society, for ascertaining the steps of the English drama, from the Mysteries celebrated in churches and by churchmen, and the final detachment from the church, and the completion of secular plays, from Ferrex and Porrex, (15) and Gammer Gurton's Needle, down to the possession of the stage by the very pieces which Shakspeare altered, remodelled and finally made his own. Elated with success and piqued by the growing interest of the problem, they have left no bookstall unsearched, no chest in a garret unopened, no file of old yellow accounts to decompose in damp and worms, so keen was the hope to discover whether the boy Shakspeare poached or not, whether he held horses at the theatre door, whether he kept school, and why he left in his will only his second-best bed to Ann Hathaway, his wife.

There is somewhat touching in the madness with which the passing age mischooses the object on which all candles shine and all eyes are turned; the care with which it registers every trifle touching

Queen Elizabeth and King James, and the Essexes, Leicesters, Burleighs and Buckinghams; and lets pass without a single valuable note the founder of another dynasty, which alone will cause the Tudor dynasty to be remembered,—the man who carries the Saxon race in him by the inspiration which feeds him, and on whose thoughts the foremost people of the world are now for some ages to be nourished, and minds to receive this and not another bias. A popular player;—nobody suspected he was the poet of the human race; and the secret was kept as faithfully from poets and intellectual men as from courtiers and frivolous people. (16) Bacon, who took the inventory of the human understanding for his times, never mentioned his name. Ben Jonson, though we have strained his few words of regard and panegyric, had no suspicion of the elastic fame whose first vibrations he was attempting. He no doubt thought the praise he has conceded to him generous, and esteemed himself, out of all question, the better poet of the two.

If it need wit to know wit, according to the proverb, Shakspeare's time should be capable of recognizing it. Sir Henry Wotton was born four years after Shakspeare, and died twenty-three years after him; and I find, among his correspondents and acquaintances, the following persons: Theodore Beza, Isaac Casaubon, Sir Philip Sidney, the Earl of Essex, Lord Bacon, Sir Walter Raleigh, John Milton, Sir Henry Vane, Isaac Walton, Dr. Donne, Abraham Cowley, Bellarmine, Charles Cotton, John Pym, John Hales, Kepler, Vieta, Albericus Gentilis, Paul Sarpi, Arminius; with all of whom exists some token of his having communicated, without enumerating many others whom doubtless he saw,—Shakspeare, Spenser, Jonson, Beaumont, Massinger, the two Herberts, Marlow, Chapman and the rest. Since the constellation of great men who appeared in Greece in the time of Pericles, there was never any such society;—yet their genius failed them to find out the best head in the universe. (17) Our poet's mask was impenetrable. You cannot see the mountain near. It took a century to make it suspected; and not until two centuries had passed, after his death, did any criticism which we think adequate begin to appear. It was not possible to write the history of Shakspeare till now; for he is the father of German literature: it was with the introduction of Shakspeare into German, by Lessing, and the translation of his works by Wieland and Schlegel, that the rapid burst of German literature was most intimately connected. It was not until the nineteenth century, whose speculative genius is a sort of living Hamlet, that the tragedy of Hamlet could find such wondering readers. (18) Now, literature, philosophy and thought are Shakspearized. His mind is the horizon beyond which, at present, we do not see. Our ears are educated to music by his rhythm. Coleridge and Goethe are the only critics who have expressed our convictions with any adequate fidelity: but there is in all cultivated minds a silent appreciation of his superlative power and beauty, which, like Christianity, qualifies the period.

The Shakspeare Society have inquired in all directions, advertised the missing facts, offered money for any information that will lead to proof,—and with what result? Beside some important illustration of the history of the English stage, to which I have adverted, they have gleaned a few facts touching the property, and dealings in regard to property, of the poet. It appears that from year to year he owned a larger share in the Blackfriars' Theatre: its wardrobe and other appurtenances were his: that he bought an estate in his native village with his earnings as writer and shareholder; that he lived in the best house in Stratford; was intrusted by his neighbors with their commissions in London, as of borrowing money, and the like; that he was a veritable farmer. About the time when he was writing Macbeth, he sues Philip Rogers, in the borough-court of Stratford, for thirty-five shillings, ten pence, for corn delivered to him at different times; and in all respects appears as a good husband, with no reputation for eccentricity or excess. He was a good-natured sort of man, an actor and shareholder in the theatre, not in any striking manner distinguished from other actors and managers. (19) I admit the importance of this information. It was well worth the pains that have been taken to procure it.

But whatever scraps of information concerning his condition these researches may have rescued, they can shed no light upon that infinite invention which is the concealed magnet of his attraction for us. We are very clumsy writers of history. We tell the chronicle of parentage, birth, birth-place, schooling, school-mates, earning of money, marriage, publication of books, celebrity, death; and when we have come to an end of this gossip, no ray of relation appears between it and the goddess-born; and it seems as if, had we dipped at random into the "Modern Plutarch," and read any other life there, it would have fitted the poems as well. (20) It is the essence of poetry to spring, like the rainbow daughter of Wonder, from the invisible, to abolish the past and refuse all history. Malone, Warburton, Dyce and Collier have wasted their oil. The famed theatres, Covent Garden, Drury Lane, the Park and Tremont have vainly assisted. Betterton, Garrick, Kemble, Kean and Macready dedicate their lives to this genius; him they crown, elucidate, obey and express. The genius knows them not. The recitation begins; one golden word leaps out immortal from all this painted pedantry and sweetly torments us with invitations to its own inaccessible homes. I remember I went once to see the Hamlet of a famed performer, the pride of the English stage; and all I then heard and all I now remember of the tragedian was that in which the tragedian had no part; simply Hamlet's question to the ghost:—

"What may this mean,
That thou, dead corse, again in complete steel
Revisit'st thus the glimpses of the moon?"

That imagination which dilates the closet he writes in to the world's dimension, crowds it with agents in rank and order, as quickly reduces the big reality to be the glimpses of the moon. (21) These tricks of his magic spoil for us the illusions of the green-room. Can any biography shed light on the localities into which the Midsummer Night's Dream admits me? Did Shakspeare confide to any notary or parish recorder, sacristan, or surrogate in Stratford, the genesis of that delicate creation? The forest of Arden, the nimble air of Scone Castle, the moonlight of Portia's villa, "the antres vast and desarts idle" of Othello's captivity,—where is the third cousin, or grand-nephew, the chancellor's file of accounts, or private letter, that has kept one word of those transcendent secrets? In fine, in this drama, as in all great works of art,—in the Cyclopæan architecture of Egypt and India, in the Phidian sculpture, the Gothic minsters, the Italian painting, the Ballads of Spain and Scotland,—the Genius draws up the ladder after him, when the creative age goes up to heaven, and gives way to a new age, which sees the works and asks in vain for a history.

Shakspeare is the only biographer of Shakspeare; and even he can tell nothing, except to the Shakspeare in us, that is, to our most apprehensive and sympathetic hour. (22) He cannot step from off his tripod and give us anecdotes of his inspirations. Read the antique documents extricated, analyzed and compared by the assiduous Dyce and Collier, and now read one of these skyey sentences,—aerolites,—which seem to have fallen out of heaven, and which not your experience but the man within the breast has accepted as words of fate, and tell me if they match; if the former account in any manner for the latter; or which gives the most historical insight into the man.

Hence, though our external history is so meagre, yet, with Shakspeare for biographer, instead of Aubrey and Rowe, we have really the information which is material; that which describes character and fortune, that which, if we were about to meet the man and deal with him, would most import us to know. We have his recorded convictions on those questions which knock for answer at every heart,—on life and death, on love, on wealth and poverty, on the prizes of life and the ways whereby we come at them; on the characters of men, and the influences, occult and open, which affect their fortunes; and on those mysterious and demoniacal powers which defy our science and which yet interweave their malice and their gift in our brightest hours. Who ever read the volume of the Sonnets without finding that the poet had there revealed, under masks that are no masks to the intelligent, the lore of friendship and of love; the confusion of sentiments in the most susceptible, and, at the same time, the most intellectual of men? What trait of his private mind has he hidden in his dramas? One can discern, in his ample pictures of the gentleman and the king, what forms and humanities pleased him; his delight in troops of friends, in large hospitality, in cheerful giving. Let Timon, let Warwick, let Antonio the merchant answer for his great heart. So far from Shakspeare's being the least known, he is the one person, in all modern history, known to us. What point of morals, of manners, of economy, of philosophy, of religion, of taste, of the conduct of life, has he not settled? What mystery has he not signified his knowledge of? What office, or function, or district of man's work, has he not remembered? What king has he not taught state, as Talma taught Napoleon? What maiden has not found him finer than her delicacy? What lover has he not outloved? What sage has he not outseen? What gentleman has he not instructed in the rudeness of his behavior?

Some able and appreciating critics think no criticism on Shakspeare valuable that does not rest purely on the dramatic merit; that he is falsely judged as poet and philosopher. I think as highly as these critics of his dramatic merit, but still think it secondary. He was a full man, who liked to talk; a brain exhaling thoughts and images, which, seeking vent, found the drama next at hand. (23) Had he been less, we should have had to consider how well he filled his place, how good a dramatist he was,—and he is the best in the world. But it turns out that what he has to say is of that weight as to withdraw some attention from the vehicle; and he is like some saint whose history is to be rendered into all languages, into verse and prose, into songs and pictures, and cut up into proverbs; so that the occasion which gave the saint's meaning the form of a conversation, or of a prayer, or of a code of laws, is immaterial compared with the universality of its application. So it fares with the wise Shakspeare and his book of life. He wrote the airs for all our modern music: he wrote the text of modern life; the text of manners: he drew the man of England and Europe; the father of the man in America; (24) he drew the man, and described the day, and what is done in it: he read the hearts of men and women, their probity, and their second thought and wiles; the wiles of innocence, and the transitions by which virtues and vices slide into their contraries: he could divide the mother's part from the father's part in the face of the child, or draw the fine demarcations of freedom and of fate: he knew the laws of repression which make the police of nature: and all the sweets and all the terrors of human lot lay in his mind as truly but as softly as the landscape lies on the eye. And the importance of this wisdom of life sinks the form, as of Drama or Epic, out of notice. 'T is like making a question concerning the paper on which a king's message is written.

Shakspeare is as much out of the category of eminent authors, as he is out of the crowd. He is inconceivably wise; the others, conceivably. A good reader can, in a sort, nestle into Plato's brain and think from thence; but not into Shakspeare's. We are still out of doors. For executive faculty, for creation, Shakspeare is unique. No man can imagine it better. He was the farthest reach of subtlety compatible with an individual self,—the subtilest of authors, and only just within the possibility of authorship. (25) With this wisdom of life is the equal endowment of imaginative and of lyric power. He clothed the creatures of his legend with form and sentiments as if they were people who had lived under his roof; and few real men have left such distinct characters as these fictions. And they spoke in language as sweet as it was fit. Yet his talents never seduced him into an ostentation, nor did he harp on one string. An omnipresent humanity co-ordinates all his faculties. Give a man of talents a story to tell, and his partiality will presently appear. He has certain observations, opinions, topics, which have some accidental prominence, and which he disposes all to exhibit. He crams this part and starves that other part, consulting not the fitness of the thing, but his fitness and strength. But Shakspeare has no peculiarity, no importunate topic; but all is duly given; no veins, no curiosities; no cow-painter, no bird-fancier, no mannerist is he: he has no discoverable egotism: the great he tells greatly; the small subordinately. He is wise without emphasis or assertion; he is strong, as nature is strong, who lifts the land into mountain slopes without effort and by the same rule as she floats a bubble in the air, and likes as well to do the one as the other. This makes that equality of power in farce, tragedy, narrative, and love-songs; a merit so incessant that each reader is incredulous of the perception of other readers.

This power of expression, or of transferring the inmost truth of things into music and verse, makes him the type of the poet and has added a new problem to metaphysics. This is that which throws him into natural history, as a main production of the globe, and as announcing new eras and ameliorations. Things were mirrored in his poetry without loss or blur: he could paint the fine with precision, the great with compass, the tragic and the comic indifferently and without any distortion or favor. He carried his powerful execution into minute details, to a hair point; finishes an eyelash or a dimple as firmly as he draws a mountain; and yet these, like nature's, will bear the scrutiny of the solar microscope.

In short, he is the chief example to prove that more or less of production, more or fewer pictures, is a thing indifferent. He had the power to make one picture. Daguerre learned how to let one flower etch its image on his plate of iodine, and then proceeds at leisure to etch a million. There are always objects; but there was never representation. Here is perfect representation, at last; and now let the world of figures sit for their portraits. No recipe can be given for the making of a Shakspeare; but the possibility of the translation of things into song is demonstrated.

His lyric power lies in the genius of the piece. The sonnets, though their excellence is lost in the splendor of the dramas, are as inimitable as they; and it is not a merit of lines, but a total merit of the piece; like the tone of voice of some incomparable person, so is this a speech of poetic beings, and any clause as unproducible now as a whole poem.

Though the speeches in the plays, and single lines, have a beauty which tempts the ear to pause on them for their euphuism, yet the sentence is so loaded with meaning and so linked with its foregoers and followers, that the logician is satisfied. His means are as admirable as his ends; every subordinate invention, by which he helps himself to connect some irreconcilable opposites, is a poem too. He is not reduced to dismount and walk because his horses are running off with him in some distant direction: he always rides.

The finest poetry was first experience; but the thought has suffered a transformation since it was an experience. Cultivated men often attain to a good degree of skill in writing verses; but it is easy to read, through their poems, their personal history: any one acquainted with the parties can name every figure; this is Andrew and that is Rachel. The sense thus remains prosaic. It is a caterpillar with wings, and not yet a butterfly. In the poet's mind the fact has gone quite over into the new element of thought, and has lost all that is exuvial. This generosity abides with Shakespeare. We say, from the truth and closeness of his pictures, that he knows the lesson by heart. Yet there is not a trace of egotism.

One more royal trait properly belongs to the poet. I mean his cheerfulness, without which no man can be a poet,—for beauty is his aim. He loves virtue, not for its obligation but for its grace: he delights in the world, in man, in woman, for the lovely light that sparkles from them. Beauty, the spirit of joy and hilarity, he sheds over the universe. Epicurus relates that poetry hath such charms that a lover might forsake his mistress to partake of them. And the true bards have been noted for their firm and cheerful temper. Homer lies in sunshine; Chaucer is glad and erect; and Saadi says, "It was rumored abroad that I was penitent; but what had I to do with repentance?" (26) Not less sovereign and cheerful,—much more sovereign and cheerful, is the tone of Shakespeare. His name suggests joy and emancipation to the heart of men. If he should appear in any company of human souls, who would not march in his troop? He touches nothing that does not borrow health and longevity from his festal style.

And now, how stands the account of man with this bard and benefactor, when, in solitude, shutting our ears to the reverberations of his fame, we seek to strike the balance? Solitude has austere lessons; it can teach us to spare both heroes and poets; and it weighs Shakespeare also, and finds him to share the halfness and imperfection of humanity.

Shakespeare, Homer, Dante, Chaucer, saw the splendor of meaning that plays over the visible world; knew that a tree had another use than for apples, and corn another than for meal, and the ball of the earth, than for tillage and roads: that these things bore a second and finer harvest to the mind, being emblems of its thoughts, and conveying in all their natural history a certain mute commentary on human life. (27) Shakespeare employed them as colors to compose his picture. He rested in their beauty; and never took the step which seemed inevitable to such genius, namely to explore the virtue which resides in these symbols and imparts this power:—what is that which they themselves say? He converted the elements which waited on his command, into entertainments. He was master of the revels to mankind. Is it not as if one should have, through majestic powers of science, the comets given into his hand, or the planets and their moons, and should draw them from their orbits to glare with the municipal fireworks on a holiday night, and advertise in all towns, "Very superior pyrotechny this evening"? Are the agents of nature, and the power to understand them, worth no more than a street serenade, or the breath of a cigar? One remembers again the trumpet-text in the Koran,—"The heavens and the earth and all that is between them, think ye we have created them in jest?" As long as the question is of talent and mental power, the world of men has not his equal to show. But when the question is, to life and its materials and its auxiliaries, how does he profit me? What does it signify? It is but a Twelfth Night, or Midsummer-Night's Dream, or Winter Evening's Tale: what signifies another picture more or less? The Egyptian verdict of the Shakespeare Societies comes to mind; that he was a jovial actor and manager. I can not marry this fact to his verse. Other admirable men have led lives in some sort of keeping with their thought; but this man, in wide contrast. Had he been less, had he reached only the common measure of great authors, of Bacon, Milton, Tasso, Cervantes, we might leave the fact in the twilight of human fate: but that this man of men, he who gave to the science of mind a new and larger subject than had ever existed, and planted the standard of humanity some furlongs forward into Chaos,—that he should not be wise for himself;—it must even go into the world's history that the best poet led an obscure and profane life, using his genius for the public amusement. (28)

Well, other men, priest and prophet, Israelite, German and Swede, beheld the same objects: they also saw through them that which was contained. And to what purpose? The beauty straightway vanished; they read commandments, all-excluding mountainous duty; an obligation, a sadness, as of piled mountains, fell on them, and life became ghastly, joyless, a pilgrim's progress, a probation, beleaguered round with doleful histories of Adam's fall and curse behind us; with doomsdays and purgatorial and penal fires before us; and the heart of the seer and the heart of the listener sank in them.

It must be conceded that these are half-views of half-men. The world still wants its poet-priest, a reconciler, who shall not trifle, with Shakespeare the player, nor shall grope in graves, with Swedenborg the mourner; but who shall see, speak, and act, with equal inspiration. For knowledge will brighten the sunshine; right is more beautiful than private affection; and love is compatible with universal wisdom. (29)

Footnotes

Note 1.

This essay was read as a lecture in Exeter Hall, in London, in June, 1848.

Perhaps it is well to bear in mind that Mr. Emerson was reared for the ministry and ordained a clergyman, and that his ancestors for several generations had exercised that office, and moreover that, in New England, up to his day, theatrical representations had been looked at with disfavor by serious and God-fearing people, and the witnessing of such by a minister would, like dancing, have been considered unbecoming indulgence. Although Mr. Emerson emancipated himself from bonds that were merely professional or artificial, he had an inbred distaste for the common amusements of society, feeling that they were unbecoming to a scholar, and that he was not adapted for them, though he was tolerant of them in other people. There was a natural earnestness, and a simple and cheerful asceticism in his early and later life. Yet once in his later life, when he had been induced to go to see Mr. and Mrs. Barney Williams in some bright comedy, he praised their acting and admitted to his daughter that he really much enjoyed theatrical performances, in spite of the feeling that they were not for him. Dancing, for instance, which he considered a proper part of youths' education, would have seemed unbecoming for himself. He says, "It shall be writ in my memoirs ... as it was writ of St. Pachonius, Pes ejus ad saltandum non est commotus omni vita sua." His staying away from theatrical entertainments was instinctive, but he was liberal in the matter and would go to see a real artist. He even went to see the performance of the beautiful dancer Fanny Elssler, although a story which has been too often repeated of his remarks to Margaret Fuller on the subject is as false as it is silly.

In Paris he saw Rachel during the Revolution of 1848, and often told his children of her fierce and splendid declamation of the Marseillaise in the theatre, holding the tricolor aloft. On London in that same year he wrote of seeing Macready in Lear, with Mrs. Butler as Cordelia. It was to see one of Shakspeare's heroes rendered by some master that he went, and probably he never was inside a theatre twenty times in his life, and, so sensitive was he to had taste or ranting, that he was usually sorry that had gone.

The rendering of Richard II. (I cannot remember by whom) more than satisfied him, and he liked to recall the actor's tones in reading this play, an especial favorite of his, to his children. Coriolanus and Julius Cæsar too he enjoyed reading to them, and he selected passages from Shakspeare for them and trained them very carefully for their recitation in school.

He saw Edwin Booth in Boston, and met him later at the house of a friend and had some talk with him. Booth later mentioned with pleasure to their host the fact that Mr. Emerson had not once alluded to his profession or performance in their conversation.

Mr. Emerson once defined the cultivated man as "one who can tell you something new and true about Shakspeare." And he read a good omen for our age in Shakspeare's acceptance: "The book only characterizes the reader. Is Shakspeare the delight of the nineteenth century? That fact only shows whereabouts we are in the ecliptic of the soul."

In writing of Great Men in 1838 in his journal, he says:—

"Swedenborg is scarce yet appreciable. Shakspeare has, for the first time, in our time found adequate criticism, if indeed he have yet found it:—Coleridge, Lamb, Schlegel, Goethe, Very, Herder.

"The great facts of history are four or five names, Homer—Phidias—Jesus—Shakspeare. One or two names more I will not add, but see what these names stand for. All civil history and all philosophy consists of endeavours more or less vain to explain these persons."

In the journal for 1843 he writes: "Plato is weak inasmuch as he is literary. Shakspeare is not literary, but the strong earth itself." Yet from another point of view he writes, "Shakspeare and Plato each sufficed for the culture of a nation."

That Shakspeare and Milton should have been born meant much to him and to mankind. "Who saw Milton, who saw Shakspeare, saw them do their best, and utter their whole heart manlike among their contemporaries."

And again, "No man can be named whose mind still acts on the cultivated intellect of England and America with an energy comparable to that of Milton. As a poet, Shakspeare undoubtedly transcends and far surpasses him in his popularity with foreign nations: but Shakspeare is a voice merely: who and what he was that sang, that sings, we know not."

Note 2.

Mr. Emerson said of Nature:—

No ray is dimmed, no atom worn,
My oldest force is good as new,
And the fresh rose on yonder thorn
Gives back the bending heavens in dew;—

and her cheerful lesson for the artist or poet was that he too could forever re-combine the old material into fresh and splendid pictures. He rejoiced that "the poet is permitted to dip his brush into the old paint-pot with which birds, flowers, the human cheek, the living rock, the broad landscape, the ocean and the eternal sky were painted," and turning from the reading of the plays he says: "'T is Shakspeare's fault that the world appears so empty. He has educated you with his painted world, and this real one seems a huckster's-shop." Again as to his true rendering of men's characters, "I value Shakspeare as a metaphysician and admire the unspoken logic which upholds the structure of Iago, Macbeth, Antony and the rest."

Note 3.

Again the ancient doctrine of the Flowing, and the modern onward and upward stream of Evolution.

Note 4.

The passive Master lent his hand
To the vast soul that o'er him planned.
"The Problem," Poems.

Note 5.

The stage was to Shakspeare his opportunity, as the Lyceum was to Emerson.

Note 6.

Henry VIII., Act V., Scene iv.

Note 7.

This estimate of the value of memory to the poet, typified by the Greeks in their making the Muses the daughters of Mnemosyne, is enlarged upon in the Essay on "Memory" in Natural History of Intellect. Mr. Emerson said once, "Of the most romantic fact the memory is more romantic," and he quotes Quintilian as saying, Quantum ingenii, tantum memoriæ.

Note 8.

In a fragment of verse written in Mr. Emerson's journal of 1831 on the yearning of the poet to enrich himself from the Treasury of the Universe, he says:—

And if to me it is not given
To fetch one ingot thence
Of that unfading gold of Heaven
His merchants may dispense,
Yet well I know the royal mine,

And know the sparkle of its ore,
Know Heaven's truth from lies that shine,—

Explored, they teach us to explore.
"Fragments on the Poet," Poems, Appendix.

Note 9.

Milton, "Il Penseroso."

Note 10.

Taine, in his History of English Literature, thus justifies Chaucer's borrowing or rendering:—

"Chaucer was capable of seeking out, in the old common forest of the middle ages, stories and legends, to replant them in his own soil and make them send out new shoots…. He has the right and power of copying and translating because by dint of retouching he impresses … his original mark. He re-creates what he imitates…. At the distance of a century and a half he has affinity with the poets of Elizabeth by his gallery of pictures."

The dates of Lydgate and Caxton show a mistake as to his use of them. Caxton, following Chaucer, when he introduced the printing-press to England, printed his poems and those of Lydgate, who was younger than Chaucer. In his House of Fame, Chaucer places, in his vision, "on a pillar higher than the rest, Homer and Livy, Dares the Phrygian, Guido Colonna, Geoffrey of Monmouth and the other historians of the war of Troy" [Taine's History of English Literature], a due recognition of his debt for Troylus and Cryseyde. As for Gower, he was Chaucer's exact contemporary and friend, and Chaucer dedicated this poem to him.

Note 11.

Kipling irreverently tells of Homer's borrowings thus:—

"When 'Omer smote 'is bloomin' lyre,
He 'd 'eard men sing by land an' sea;

An' what he thought 'e might require,
'E went an' took—the same as me!"
And says of his humble audience:—

"They knew 'e stole; 'e knew they knowed.
They did n't tell, nor make a fuss,
But winked at 'Omer down the road,
An' 'e winked back—the same as us!"

Note 12.

Dr. Holmes's remark with regard to the preceding page is: "The reason why Emerson has so much to say on this subject of borrowing, especially when treating of Plato and Shakspeare, is obvious enough. He was arguing his own cause—not defending himself," etc. In Letters and Social Aims, Mr. Emerson discusses Quotation and Originality.

Note 13.

Mr. Emerson had tender associations with the Book of Common Prayer. His mother had been brought up in the Episcopal communion, and the prayer-book of her youth was always by her, though after her marriage she attended her husband's church. [In Mr. Cabot's Memoir, vol. ii. p. 572, see Mr. Emerson's letter on his mother's death.]

Note 14.

Landor says of these borrowings of Shakspeare, "He breathed upon dead bodies and brought them to life."

Note 15.

The princes Ferrex and Porrex, brothers and rivals for the ancient British throne, are characters in the tragedy Gorboduc by Norton and Sackville, to which the date 1561 is assigned. Gammer Gurton's Needle is a comedy of the same period.

Note 16.

Journal, 1864. "Shakspeare puts us all out. No theory will account for him. He neglected his works, perchance he did not know their value? Ay, but he did; witness the sonnets. He went into company as a listener, hiding himself, [Greek]; was only remembered by all as a delightful companion."

Note 17.

England's genius filled all measure
Of heart and soul, of strength and pleasure,
Gave to the mind its emperor,
And life was larger than before:
Nor sequent centuries could hit
Orbit and sum of Shakspeare's wit.
The men who lived with him became
Poets, for the air was fame.
"The Solution," Poems.

Note 18.

While writing this, Mr. Emerson was surrounded by persons paralyzed for active life in the common world by the doubts of conscience or entangled in over-fine-spun webs of their intellect. [back]

Note 19.

Journal, 1837. "I either read or inferred to-day in the Westminster Review that Shakspeare was not a popular man in his day. How true and wise. He sat alone and walked alone, a visionary poet, and came with his piece, modest but discerning, to the players, and was too glad to get it received, whilst he was too superior not to see its transcendent claims."

Note 20.

The following is the "Exordium of a lecture on Poetry and Eloquence," given in London in 1848:

"Shakspeare is nothing but a large utterance. We cannot find that anything in his age was more worth telling than anything in ours; nor give any account of his existence, but only the fact that there was a wonderful symbolizer and expresser, who has no rival in the ages, and who has thrown an accidental lustre over his time and subject."

In the lecture on "Works and Days" he wrote, "Shakspeare made his Hamlet as a bird weaves its nest." And in that on "Inspiration" in Letters and Social Aims: "Shakspeare seems to you miraculous, but the wonderful juxtapositions, parallelisms, transfers, which his genius effected, were all to him locked together as links of a chain, and the mode precisely as conceivable and familiar to higher intelligence as the index-making of the literary hack."

Journal, 1838. "Read Lear yesterday and Hamlet to-day with new wonder and mused much on the great Soul in the broad continuous daylight of these poems. Especially I wonder at the perfect reception this wit and immense knowledge of life and intellectual superiority find in us all in connection with our utter incapacity to produce anything like it. The superior tone of Hamlet in all the conversations how perfectly preserved, without any mediocrity, much less any dulness in the other speakers.

"How real the loftiness! an inborn gentleman; and above that, an exalted intellect. What incessant growth and plenitude of thought,—pausing on itself never an instant, and each sally of wit sufficient to save the play. How true then and unerring the earnest of the dialogue, as when Hamlet talks with the Queen. How terrible his discourse! What less can be said of the perfect mastery, as by a superior being, of the conduct of the drama, as the free introduction of this capital advice to the players; the commanding good sense which never retreats except before the Godhead which inspires certain passages—the more I think of it, the more I wonder. I will think nothing impossible to man. No Parthenon, no sculpture, no picture, no architecture can be named beside this. All this is perfectly visible to me and to many,—the wonderful truth and mastery of this work, of these works,—yet for our lives could not I, or any man, or all men, produce anything comparable to one scene in Hamlet or Lear. With all my admiration of this life-like picture, set me to producing a match for it, and I should instantly depart into mouthing rhetoric…. One other fact Shakspeare presents us; that not by books are great poets made. Somewhat—and much, he unquestionably owes to his books; but you could not find in his circumstances the history of his poems. It was made without hands in his invisible world. A mightier magic than any learning, the deep logic of cause and effect he studied: its roots were cast so deep, therefore it flung out its branches so high."

Note 21.

Mr. Edwin P. Whipple, writing in Harper's Monthly in 1882, relates how in a long drive with Mr. Emerson, after a lecture, "The conversation at last drifted to contemporary actors who assumed to personate leading characters in Shakspeare's greatest plays. Had I ever seen an actor who satisfied me when he pretended to be Hamlet or Othello, Lear or Macbeth? Yes, I had seen the elder Booth in these characters. Though not perfect, he approached nearer to perfection than any other actor I knew—

"'Ah,' said Emerson, [after] the three minutes I consumed in eulogizing Booth,... 'I see you are one of the happy mortals who are capable of being carried away by an actor of Shakspeare. Now, whenever I visit the theatre to witness the performance of one of his dramas, I am carried away by the poet. I went last Tuesday to see Macready in Hamlet. I got along very well until he came to the passage:—

"thou, dead corse, again, in complete steel,
Revisit'st thus the glimpses of the moon:"—

and then actor, theatre, all vanished in view of that solving and dissolving imagination, which could reduce this big globe and all it inherits into mere "glimpses of the moon." The play went on, but, absorbed in this one thought of the mighty master, I paid no heed to it.'

"What specially impressed me, as Emerson was speaking, was his glance at our surroundings as he slowly uttered, 'glimpses of the moon,' for here above us was the same moon which must have given birth to Shakspeare's thought.... Afterward, in his lecture on Shakspeare, Emerson made use of the thought suggested in our ride by moonlight. He said, 'That imagination which dilates the closet he writes in to the world's dimensions, crowds it with agents in rank and order, as quickly reduces the big reality to be the "glimpses of the moon."'... In the printed lecture, there is one sentence declaring the absolute insufficiency of any actor, in any theatre, to fix attention on himself while uttering Shakspeare's words, which seems to me the most exquisite statement ever made of the magical suggestiveness of Shakspeare's expression. I have often quoted it, but it will bear quotation again and again, as the best prose sentence ever written on this side of the Atlantic: 'The recitation begins; one golden word leaps out immortal from all this painted pedantry, and sweetly torments us with invitations to its own inaccessible homes.'"

Note 22.

The little Shakspeare in the maiden's heart
Makes Romeo of a ploughboy on his cart;
Opens the eye to Virtue's starlike meed
And gives persuasion to a gentle deed.
"The Enchanter," Poems, Appendix.

Note 23.

And yet perhaps there is some truth in Dr. Richard Garnett's word in his Life of Emerson:

"Emerson is incapable of contemplating Shakspeare with the eye of a dramatic critic."

Just after Mr. Emerson settled in Concord he read with great pleasure Henry Taylor's play Philip van Artevelde, then recently published. He wrote in his journal for 1835:—

"I think Taylor's poem is the best light we have ever had upon the genius of Shakspeare. We have made a miracle of Shakspeare, a haze of light instead of a guiding torch, by accepting unquestioned all the tavern stories about his want of education, and total unconsciousness. The internal evidence all the time is irresistible that he was no such person. He was a man, like this Taylor, of strong sense and of great cultivation; an excellent Latin scholar, and of extensive and select reading, so as to have formed his theories of many historical characters with as much clearness as Gibbon or Niebuhr or Goethe. He wrote for intelligent persons, and wrote with intention. He had Taylor's strong good sense, and added to it his own wonderful facility of execution which aerates and sublimes all language the moment he uses it, or more truly, animates every word."

Note 24.

Lowell, in one of his essays, calls attention to the survival in New England of the type of face of the English in Queen Elizabeth's day even more than in the mother country, and also to the old English expressions, obsolete in England, but still current on New England farms.

Note 25.

Journal, 1838. fills us with wonder the first time we approach him. We go away, and work and think, for years, and come again,—he astonishes us anew. Then, having drank deeply and saturated us with his genius, we lose sight of him for another period of years. By and by we return, and there he stands immeasurable as at first. We have grown wiser, but only that we should see him wiser than ever. He resembles a high mountain which the traveller sees in the morning, and thinks he shall quickly near it and pass it, and leave it behind. But he journeys all day till noon, till night. There still is the dim mountain close by him, having scarce altered its bearings since the morning light."

Note 26.

And yet it seemeth not to me
That the high gods love tragedy;
For Saadi sat in the sun,
And thanks was his contrition;

And yet his runes he rightly read,
And to his folk his message sped.
"Saadi," Poems.

Note 27.

This image appears in "The Apology" in the Poems.

Note 28.

The Puritan shrinking from the form in which the great poet embodied his thought or oracles or dreams still appears in the journal of 1852, yet, contrasted to the dismal seers, Shakspeare is well-nigh pardoned his levity.

"There was never anything more excellent came from a human brain than the plays of Shakspeare, bating only that they were plays. The Greek has a real advantage of them in the degree in which his dramas had a religious office. Could the priest look him in the face without blenching?"

In 1839 Mr. Emerson had written:—

"It is in the nature of things that the highest originality must be moral. The only person who can be entirely independent of this fountain of literature and equal to it, must be a prophet in his own proper person. Shakspeare, the first literary genius of the world, leans on the Bible: his poetry supposes it. If we examine this brilliant influence, Shakspeare, as it lies in our minds, we shall find it reverent, deeply indebted to the traditional morality, in short, compared with the tone of the prophets, Secondary. On the other hand, the Prophets do not imply the existence of Shakspeare or Homer,—to no books or arts,—only to dread Ideas and emotions."

Note 29.

All through his life Mr. Emerson felt increasing thankfulness for "the Spirit of joy which Shakspeare had shed over the Universe." In 1864 he wrote:—

"When I read Shakspeare, as lately, I think the criticism and study of him to be in their infancy. The wonder grows of his long obscurity:—how could you hide the only man that ever wrote from all men who delight in reading?"

And again he wrote: "Your criticism is profane. Shakspeare by Shakspeare. The poet in his interlunation is a critic,"—that is, his worst is criticised by his best performance.

Journal, 1864. "How to say it I know not, but I know that the point of praise of Shakspeare is the pure poetic power: he is the chosen closet companion, who can, at any moment, by incessant surprises, work the miracle of mythologizing every fact of the common life; as snow, or moonlight, or the level rays of sunrise lend a momentary glow to Pump and wood-pile."

And again: 1836. "It is easy to solve the problem of individual existence. Why Milton, Shakspeare, or Canova should be there is reason enough. But why the million should exist drunk with the opium of Time and Custom does not appear."

But even Shakspeare must not be idolized. The soul must rely on itself, that is, on the universal fountain of beauty, wisdom and goodness to which it is open. So thus he draws the moral:—

1838. "The indisposition of men to go back to the source and mix with Deity is the reason of degradation and decay. Education is expended in the measurement and imitation of effects in the study of Shakspeare, for example, as itself a perfect being—instead of using Shakspeare merely as an effect of which the cause is with every scholar. Thus the college becomes idolatrous—a temple full of idols. Shakspeare will never be made by the study of Shakspeare. I know not how directions for greatness can be given, yet greatness may be inspired."

Feb. 1838. "Consider too how Shakspeare and Milton are formed. They are just such men as we all are to contemporaries, and none suspected their superiority,—but after all were dead, and a generation or two besides, it is discovered that they surpass all. Each of us then take the same moral to himself."

Index of Contents
To the Memory of My Beloved, the Author, Mr William Shakespeare, & What He Hath Left Us by Ben Jonson
Shakespeare by Matthew Arnold
An Epitaph On The Admirable Dramatic Poet W. Shakespeare by John Milton
Shakespeare by Henry Wadsworth Longfellow
Elegy On Mr. William Shakespeare by William Basse
Shakespeare by Vachel Lindsay
The Spirit of Shakespeare by George Meredith
To Shakespeare by Lord Alfred Douglas
To Shakespeare (I) by Frances Anne Kemble
To Shakespeare (II) by Frances Anne Kemble
To Shakespeare (III) by Frances Anne Kemble
Shakespeare and Milton by Walter Savage Landor
A Shakespeare Memorial by Alfred Austin
Shakespeare by Mathilde Blind
Shakespeare by Robert Crawford
Shakespeare by Thomas Gent
Shakespeare's Mourners by John Bannister Tabb
Shakespeare by Philip Henry Savage
Shakespeare by Lucretia Maria Davidson
Shakespeare by Frederick George Scott
Shakespeare's Kingdom by Alfred Noyes
Shakespeare 1916 by Sir Ronald Ross
Song, In Imitation of Shakspeare's by James Beattie
In A Letter To C. P. Esq. In Imitation o Shakspeare by William Cowper
Shakspeare. (An Ode For His Three-Hundredth Birthday) by Martin Farquhar Tupper
On The Site of A Mulberry-Tree; Planted By Wm. Shakspeare; Felled By The Rev. F. Gastrell by Dante Gabriel Rossetti

To The Memory of My Beloved, The Author, Mr William Shakespeare, And What He Hath Left Us by Ben Jonson

To draw no envy, Shakespeare, on thy name
Am I thus ample to thy book and fame;
While I confess thy writings to be such
As neither Man nor Muse can praise too much.
'Tis true, and all men's suffrage. But these ways
Were not the paths I meant unto thy praise;
For silliest ignorance on these may light,
Which when it sounds at best but echoes right;
Or blind affection, which doth ne'er advance
The truth, but gropes, and urges all by chance;
Or crafty malice might pretend this praise,
And think to ruin where it seemed to raise.
These are as some infamous bawd or whore
Should praise a matron. What could hurt her more?
But thou art proof against them, and indeed
Above th' ill fortune of them, or the need.

I therefore will begin: Soul of the Age!
The applause, delight, the wonder of our stage!
My Shakespeare, rise; I will not lodge thee by
Chaucer, or Spenser, or bid Beaumont lie
A little further, to make thee a room:
Thou art a monument without a tomb,
And art alive still, while thy book doth live,
And we have wits to read, and praise to give.
That I not mix thee so, my brain excuses,
I mean with great but disproportioned Muses,
For if I thought my judgement were of years,
I should commit thee surely with thy peers,
And tell how far thou didst our Lyly outshine,
Or sporting Kyd, or Marlowe's mighty line.
And though thou hadst small Latin and less Greek,
From thence to honour thee I would not seek
For names; but call forth thundering Aeschylus,
Euripides, and Sophocles to us,
Pacuvius, Accius, him of Cordova dead,
To live again, to hear thy buskin tread,
And shake a stage; or, when thy socks were on,
Leave thee alone for the comparison
Of all that insolent Greece or haughty Rome
Sent forth, or since did from their ashes come.
Triumph, my Britain, thou hast one to show
To whom all scenes of Europe homage owe.
He was not of an age, but for all time!
And all the Muses still were in their prime
When, like Apollo, he came forth to warm
Our ears, or, like a Mercury, to charm!
Nature herself was proud of his designs,
And joyed to wear the dressing of his lines!
Which were so richly spun, and woven so fit,
As, since, she will vouchsafe no other wit.
The merry Greek, tart Aristophanes,
Neat Terence, witty Plautus, now not please;
But antiquated and deserted lie,
As they were not of Nature's family.
Yet must I not give Nature all; thy art,
My gentle Shakespeare, must enjoy a part.
For though the poet's matter nature be,
His art doth give the fashion; and that he
Who casts to write a living line must sweat
(Such as thine are) and strike the second heat
Upon the Muses' anvil; turn the same,
And himself with it, that he thinks to frame,
Or for the laurel he may gain a scorn;
For a good poet's made as well as born.
And such wert thou. Look how the father's face
Lives in his issue, even so the race
Of Shakespeare's mind and manners brightly shines

In his well turned and true-filed lines:
In each of which he seems to shake a lance,
As brandished at the eyes of ignorance.
Sweet swan of Avon! what a sight it were
To see thee in our waters yet appear,
And make those flights upon the banks of Thames,
That did so take Eliza and our James!
But stay, I see thee in the hemisphere
Advanced, and made a constellation there:
Shine forth, thou Star of Poets, and with rage,
Or influence, chide or cheer the drooping stage,
Which, since thy flight from hence, hath mourned like night,
And despairs day, but for thy volume's light.

Shakespeare by Matthew Arnold

Others abide our question. Thou art free.
We ask and ask—Thou smilest and art still,
Out-topping knowledge. For the loftiest hill,
Who to the stars uncrowns his majesty,

Planting his steadfast footsteps in the sea,
Making the heaven of heavens his dwelling-place,
Spares but the cloudy border of his base
To the foil'd searching of mortality;

And thou, who didst the stars and sunbeams know,
Self-school'd, self-scann'd, self-honour'd, self-secure,
Didst tread on earth unguess'd at.—Better so!

All pains the immortal spirit must endure,
All weakness which impairs, all griefs which bow,
Find their sole speech in that victorious brow

An Epitaph On The Admirable Dramatic Poet W. Shakespeare by John Milton

What needs my Shakespeare for his honored bones
The labor of an age in piled stones?
Or that his hallowed reliques should be hid
Under a star-ypointing pyramid?
Dear son of Memory, great heir of Fame,
What need'st thou such weak witness of thy name?
Thou in our wonder and astonishment
Hast built thy self a livelong monument.
For whilst, to th' shame of slow-endeavoring art,
Thy easy numbers flow, and that each heart
Hath from the leaves of thy unvalued book

Those Delphic lines with deep impression took,
Then thou, our fancy of itself bereaving,
Dost make us marble with too much conceiving,
And so sepulchred in such pomp dost lie
That kings for such a tomb would wish to die.

Shakespeare by Henry Wadsworth Longfellow

A vision as of crowded city streets,
With human life in endless overflow;
Thunder of thoroughfares; trumpets that blow
To battle; clamor, in obscure retreats,
Of sailors landed from their anchored fleets;
Tolling of bells in turrets, and below
Voices of children, and bright flowers that throw
O'er garden-walls their intermingled sweets!
This vision comes to me when I unfold
The volume of the Poet paramount,
Whom all the Muses loved, not one alone;—
Into his hands they put the lyre of gold,
And, crowned with sacred laurel at their fount,
Placed him as Musagetes on their throne.

Elegy On Mr. William Shakespeare by William Basse

Renowned Spenser, lie a thought more nigh
To learned Chaucer, and rare Beaumont lie
A little nearer Spenser, to make room
For Shakespeare in your threefold, fourfold tomb.
To lodge all four in one bed, make a shift
Until Doomsday, for hardly will a fift
Betwixt this day and that by Fate be slain,
For whom your curtains may be drawn again.
If your precedency in death doth bar
A fourth place in your sacred sepulchre,
Under this carved marble of thine own,
Sleep, rare tragedian, Shakespeare, sleep alone;
Thy unmolested peace, unshared cave
Possess as lord, not tenant of thy grave,
That unto us and others it may be
Honour hereafter to be laid by thee.

Shakespeare by Vachel Lindsay

Would that in body and spirit Shakespeare came

Visible emperor of the deeds of Time,
With Justice still the genius of his rhyme,
Giving each man his due, each passion grace,
Impartial as the rain from Heaven's face
Or sunshine from the heaven-enthroned sun.
Sweet Swan of Avon, come to us again.
Teach us to write, and writing, to be men.

The Spirit of Shakespeare by George Meredith

Thy greatest knew thee, Mother Earth; unsoured
He knew thy sons. He probed from hell to hell
Of human passions, but of love deflowered
His wisdom was not, for he knew thee well.
Thence came the honeyed corner at his lips,
The conquering smile wherein his spirit sails
Calm as the God who the white sea-wave whips,
Yet full of speech and intershifting tales,
Close mirrors of us: thence had he the laugh
We feel is thine: broad as ten thousand beeves
At pasture! thence thy songs, that winnow chaff
From grain, bid sick Philosophy's last leaves
Whirl, if they have no response-they enforced
To fatten Earth when from her soul divorced.

To Shakespeare by Lord Alfred Douglas

Most tuneful singer, lover tenderest,
Most sad, most piteous, and most musical,
Thine is the shrine more pilgrim-worn than all
The shrines of singers; high above the rest
Thy trumpet sounds most loud, most manifest.
Yet better were it if a lonely call
Of woodland birds, a song, a madrigal,
Were all the jetsam of thy sea's unrest.

For now thy praises have become too loud
On vulgar lips, and every yelping cur
Yaps thee a paean; the whiles little men,
Not tall enough to worship in a crowd,
Spit their small wits at thee. Ah! better then
The broken shrine, the lonely worshipper.

To Shakespeare (I) by Frances Anne Kemble

If from the height of that celestial sphere
Where now thou dwell'st, spirit powerful and sweet!
Thou yet canst love the race that sojourn here,
How must thou joy, with pleasure not unmeet
For thy exalted state, to know how dear
Thy memory is held throughout the earth,
Beyond the favoured land that gave thee birth.
E'en in thy seat in Heaven, thou may'st receive
Thanks, praise, and love, and wonder ever new,
From human hearts, who in thy verse perceive
All that humanity calls good and true;
Nor dost thou for each mortal blemish grieve,
They from thy glorious works have fall'n away,
As from thy soul its outward form of clay.

To Shakespeare (II) by Frances Anne Kemble

Oft, when my lips I open to rehearse
Thy wondrous spells of wisdom and of power,
And that my voice and thy immortal verse
On listening ears and hearts I mingled pour,
I shrink dismayed—and awful doth appear
The vain presumption of my own weak deed;
Thy glorious spirit seems to mine so near,
That suddenly I tremble as I read—
Thee an invisible auditor I fear:
Oh, if it might be so, my master dear!
With what beseeching would I pray to thee,
To make me equal to my noble task,
Succour from thee, how humbly would I ask,
Thy worthiest works to utter worthily.

To Shakespeare (III) by Frances Anne Kemble

Shelter and succour such as common men
Afford the weaker partners of their fate,
Have I derived from thee—from thee, most great
And powerful genius! whose sublime control,
Still from thy grave governs each human soul,
That reads the wondrous records of thy pen.
From sordid sorrows thou hast set me free,
And turned from want's grim ways my tottering feet,
And to sad empty hours, given royally,
A labour, than all leisure far more sweet:
The daily bread, for which we humbly pray,
Thou gavest me as if I were thy child,
And still with converse noble, wise, and mild,

Charmed from despair my sinking soul away;
Shall I not bless the need, to which was given
Of all the angels in the host of heaven,
Thee, for my guardian, spirit strong and bland!
Lord of the speech of my dear native land!

Shakespeare and Milton by Walter Savage Landor

The tongue of England, that which myriads
Have spoken and will speak, were paralyz'd
Hereafter, but two mighty men stand forth
Above the flight of ages, two alone;
One crying out,
All nations spoke through me.
The other:
True; and through this trumpet burst God's word;
The fall of Angels, and the doom
First of immortal, then of mortal, Man.
Glory! be glory! not to me, to God.

A Shakespeare Memorial by Alfred Austin

Why should we lodge in marble or in bronze
Spirits more vast than earth, or sea, or sky?
Wiser the silent worshipper that cons
Their words for wisdom that will never die.
Unto the favourite of the passing hour
Erect the statue and parade the bust;
Whereon decisive Time will slowly shower
Oblivion's refuse and disdainful dust.
The Monarchs of the Mind, self-sceptred Kings,
Need no memento to transmit their name:
Throned on their thoughts and high imaginings,
They are the Lords, not sycophants of Fame.
Raise pedestals to perishable stuff:
Gods for themselves are monuments enough.

Shakespeare by Mathilde Blind

Yearning to know herself for all she was,
Her passionate clash of warring good and ill,
Her new life ever ground in Death's old mill,
With every delicate detail and en masse,—
Blind Nature strove. Lo, then it came to pass,
That Time, to work out her unconscious Will,

Once wrought the Mind which she had groped for still,
And she beheld herself as in a glass.

The world of men, unrolled before our sight,
Showed like a map, where stream and waterfall
And village-cradling vale and cloud-capped height
Stand faithfully recorded, great and small;
For Shakespeare was, and at his touch, with light
Impartial as the Sun's, revealed the All.

Shakespeare by Robert Crawford

And what think ye of Shakespeare? 'Twas not he
Of Stratford is the lord of England's lyre;
Ay, not the rustic lad, whoe'er it be,
Momentous in his doing and desire.
But little Latin and less Greek? Ah, no!
It was a teeming scholar who enwrought
The wondrous pages where the wisest go
For th' culmination of the life of thought.
No jovial actor, no mere Shakescene who
Found it so hard his dear name to indite,
The marvellous pictures of our nature drew
And limned the universe in his delight.
We do not know the man; but 'twas not Will
Whose hand is on the lyre of England still.

Shakespeare by Thomas Gent

While o'er this pageant of sublunar things
Oblivion spreads her unrelenting wings,
And sweeps adown her dark unebbing tide
Man, and his mightiest monuments of pride-
Alone, aloft, immutable, sublime,
Star-like, ensphered above the track of time,
Great SHAKSPEARE beams with undiminish'd ray.
His bright creations sacred from decay,
Like Nature's self, whose living form he drew,
Though still the same, still beautiful and new.

He came, untaught in academic bowers,
A gift to Glory from the Sylvan powers:
But what keen Sage, with all the science fraught,
By elder bards or later critics taught,
Shall count the cords of his mellifluous shell,
Span the vast fabric of his fame, and tell
By what strange arts he bade the structure rise-

On what deep site the strong foundation lies?
This, why should scholiasts labour to reveal?
We all can answer it, we all can feel,
Ten thousand sympathies, attesting, start-
For SHAKSPEARE'S Temple, is the human heart!

Lord of a throne which mortal ne'er shall share-
Despot adored! he rales and revels there.
Who but has found, where'er his track hath been,
Through life's oft shifting, multifarious scene,
Still at his side the genial Bard attend,
His loved companion, counsellor, and friend!

The Thespian Sisters nurtured in the schools
Of Greece and Rome, and long coerced by rules,
Scarce moved the inmates of their native hearth
With tiny pathos and with trivial mirth,
Till She, great muse of daring enterprise,
Delighted ENGLAND! saw her SHAKSPEARE rise!

Then, first aroused in that appointed hour,
The Tragic Muse confess'd th' inspiring power;
Sudden before the startled earth she stood,
A giant spectre, weeping tears and blood;
Guilt shrunk appall'd, Despair embraced his shroud,
And Terror shriek'd, and Pity sobb'd aloud;-
Then, first Thalia with dilated ken
And quicken'd footstep pierced the walks of men;
Then Folly blush'd, Vice fled the general hiss,
Delight met Reason with a loving kiss;
At Satire's glance Pride smooth'd his low'ring crest,
The Graces weaved the dance.-And last and best
Came Momus down in Falstaff's form to earth.
To make the world one universe of mirth!

Such Sympathies the glorious Bard endear!
Thus fair he walks in Man's diurnal sphere.
But when, upborne on bright Invention's wings.
He dares the realms of uncreated things,
Forms more divine, more dreadful, start to view,
Than ever Hades or Olympus knew.
Round the dark cauldron, terrible and fell,
The midnight Witches breathe the songs of hell;
Delighted Ariel wings his fiery way
To whirl the storm, the wheeling Orbs to stay;
Then bathes in honey-dews, and sleeps in flowers;
Meanwhile, young Oberon, girt with shadowy powers,
Pursues o'er Ocean's verge the pale cold Moon,
Or hymns her, riding in her highest noon.

Thus graced, thus glorified, shall SHAKSPEARE crave

The Sculptor's skill, the pageant of the grave?
HE needs it not-but Gratitude demands
This votive offering at his Country's hands.
Haply, e'er now, from blissful bowers on high,
From some Parnassus of the empyreal sky,
Pleased, o'er this dome the gentle Spirit bends,
Accepts the gift, and hails us as his friends-
Yet smiles, perchance, to think when envious Time
O'er Bust and Urn shall bid his ivies climb,
When Palaces and Pyramids shall fall-
HIS PAGE SHALL TRIUMPH-still surviving all-
'Till Earth itself, 'like breath upon the wind,'
Shall melt away, 'nor leave a rack behind!'

Shakespeare's Mourners by John Bannister Tabb

I saw the grave of Shakespeare in a dream,
And round about it grouped a wondrous throng,
His own majestic mourners, who belong
Forever to the Stage of Life, and seem
The rivals of reality. Supreme
Stood Hamlet, as erewhile the graves among,
Mantled in thought: and sad Ophelia sung
The same swan-dirge she chanted in the stream.
Othello, dark in destiny's eclipse,
Laid on the tomb a lily. Near him wept
Dejected Constance. Fair Cordelia's lips
Moved prayerfully the while her father slept,
And each and all, inspired of vital breath,
Kept vigil o'er the sacred spoils of death.

Shakespeare by Philip Henry Savage

Through time untimed, if truly great, a Name
Reverence compels and, that forgotten, shame.
But in the stress of living you shall scan,
Yea, touch and censure, great or small, the Man.

Shakespeare by Lucretia Maria Davidson

Shakspeare!' with all thy faults, (and few have more,)
I love thee still,' and still will con thee o'er.
Heaven, in compassion to man's erring heart,
Gave thee of virtue — then, of vice a part,
Lest we, in wonder here, should bow before thee,

Break God's commandment, worship, and adore thee:
But admiration now, and sorrow join;
His works we reverence, while we pity thine.

Shakespeare by Frederick George Scott

Unseen in the great minister dome of time,
Whose shafts are centuries, its spangled roof
The vaulted universe, our master sits,
And organ-voices like a far-off chime
Roll thro' the aisles of thought. The sunlight flits

From arch to arch, and, as he sits aloof,
Kings, heroes, priests, in concourse vast, sublime,
Glances of love and cries from battle-field,
His wizard power breathes on the living air.
Warm faces gleam and pass, child, woman, man,

In the long multitude; but he, concealed,
Our bard eludes us, vainly each face we scan,
It is not he; his features are not there;
But, being thus hid, his greatness is revealed.

Shakespeare's Kingdom by Alfred Noyes

When Shakespeare came to London
He met no shouting throngs;
He carried in his knapsack
A scroll of quiet songs.

No proud heraldic trumpet
Acclaimed him on his way;
Their court and camp have perished;
The songs live on for ay.

Nobody saw or heard them,
But, all around him there,
Spirits of light and music
Went treading the April air.

He passed like any pedlar,
Yet he had wealth untold.
The galleons of th' armada
Could not contain his gold.

The kings rode on to darkness.
In England's conquering hour,

Unseen arrived her splendour;
Unknown, her conquering power.

Shakespeare 1916 by Sir Ronald Ross

Now when the sinking Sun reeketh with blood,
And the gore-gushing vapors rent by him
Rend him and bury him: now the World is dim
As when great thunders gather for the flood,
And in the darkness men die where they stood,
And dying slay, or scatter'd limb from limb
Cease in a flash where mad-eyed cherubim
Of Death destroy them in the night and mud:
When landmarks vanish—murder is become
A glory—cowardice, conscience— and to lie,
A law—to govern, but to serve a time:—
We dying, lifting bloodied eyes and dumb,
Behold the silver star serene on high,
That is thy spirit there, O Master Mind sublime.

Song, In Imitation of Shakspeare's by James Beattie

I
Blow, blow, thou vernal gale!
Thy balm will not avail
To ease my aching breast;
Though thou the billows smooth,
Thy murmurs cannot soothe
My weary soul to rest.

II
Flow, flow, thou tuneful stream!
Infuse the easy dream
Into the peaceful soul;
But thou canst not compose
The tumult of my woes,
Though soft thy waters roll.

III
Blush, blush, ye fairest flowers!
Beauties surpassing yours
My Rosalind adorn;
Nor is the Winter's blast,
That lays your glories waste,
So killing as her scorn.

IV

Breathe, breathe, ye tender lays,
That linger down the maze
Of yonder winding grove;
O let your soft control
Bend her relenting soul
To pity and to love.

V
Fade, fade, ye flowerets fair!
Gales, fan no more the air!
Ye streams, forget to glide;
Be hush'd each vernal strain;
Since nought can soothe my pain,
Nor mitigate her pride.

In A Letter To C. P. Esq. In Imitation Of Shakspeare by William Cowper

Trust me the meed of praise, dealt thriftily
From the nice scale of judgement, honours more
Than does the lavish and o'erbearing tide
Of profuse courtesy. Not all the gems
Of India's richest soil at random spread
O'er the gay vesture of some glittering dame,
Give such alluring vantage to the person,
As the scant lustre of a few, with choice
And comely guise of ornament disposed.

Shakspeare. (An Ode For His Three-Hundredth Birthday) by Martin Farquhar Tupper

I.
Immortal! risen to thy Rest,
Immortal! throned among the Blest,
Immortal! long an heir sublime
Of realms outreaching space and time,—
How shall we dare, or hope, to raise
A fitting homage of high praise
To please thy Spirit, sphered on high
Where planets roll and comets fly?
How may not thy pure fame be marr'd
By the damp breath of earthly bard,
Presuming in his zeal too bold
To gild the bright refinèd gold?
Or how canst thou, fill'd with God's love,
And tranced among the saints above,
Endure that men should seem and be
Idolaters in praise of thee!
Forgive our love, forgive our zeal,—

We cannot guess how spirits feel;
And may our homage offered thus
Please HIM who made both thee, and us!

II.
Immortal also on this darker Earth
As in those brighter spheres,
Now will we consecrate our Shakespeare's birth,
This day three hundred years!
And so from age to age for evermore
His glory shall extend,
With men of every land the wide world o'er,
Till Time itself shall end!
For, he is our's; and well with pride and joy
England may bless her son,
The Stratford scholar and the Warwick boy
That every crown hath won!
Let others boast their wisest and their best,
To each a prize may fall;
Genius gives one apiece to all the rest,
But Shakspeare claims them all!

III.
A Homer, in majestic eloquence,
A Terence, for keen wit and stinging sense,
Brighter than Pindar in his loftiest flight,
Darker than Æschylus for deeds of night,
An Ovid, in the story-pictured page,
A Juvenal, to lash the vicious age,
Graceful as Horace and more skill'd to please,
Tender as pity-stirring Sophocles,
Free as Anacreon, as Martial neat,
Than Virgil's self more delicately sweet,—
O let those ancients bend before Thee now,
And pile their many chaplets on one brow!—
Milton was great, and of divinest song,
Spenser melodious, Chaucer rough and strong,—
The vigorous Dryden, and the classic Gray,
And awful Danté, soaring far away,
Schiller and Göethe, stirring up the strife,
And Molière, dropping laughter into life,
Burns, a full spring of nature, Hood of wit,
And Tennyson, most rare and exquisite,
To each and all belongs the laurell'd crown,
And woe to him who drags their honours down,—
Yet, Shakspeare, thou wert all these lights combined,
O manysided crystal of mankind!

IV.
The jealous Moor, the thoughtful Dane,
The witty rare fat knight,

And grand old Lear half-insane,
And fell Iago's spite,
And Romeo's love, and Tybalt's hate,
And Bolinbroke in regal state,
And he that murdered sleep,—
And ruthless Shylock's bloody bond,
And Prosper with his broken wand
Long buried fathoms deep!
Frank Juliet too,— and that soft pair
Helen and Hermia, lilies fair
As growing on one stem,
Love-crazed Ophelia, drown'd ah! drown'd,
And wanton Cleopatra, crown'd
With Egypt's diadem;
The young Miranda most admired,
Cordelia's filial heart,
Sly Beatrice with wit inspired,
And Ariel's tricksey part,
Fair Rosalind,— sweet banishèd,
And gentle Desdemona — dead!—
Ay these, all these, and crowds beside,
Heroes, jesters, courtiers, clowns,
Girls in grief, or kings in pride,
Threats and crimes, and jokes, and frowns,
Witches, fairies, ghosts, and elves,
All our fancies, all ourselves,—
O! thou hast pictured with thy pen
All phases of all hearts of men,
And in thy various page survives
The Panorama of our lives!

V.
O Paragon unthought before,
O miracle of selftaught lore,
A universe of wit and worth,
The admirable Man of earth,
There is nor thing, nor thought, nor whim,
Untouch'd and unadorn'd by him;
No theme unsung, no truth untold
Of Earth's museum, new or old:
All Nature's hidden things he saw,
Intuitive to every law;
Glancing with supernal scan
At all the knowledge spelt by man;
While, for each rule and craft of Art
He grasp'd it amply, whole and part:
Like travel-wise Ulysses well he knew
Peoples and cities, men and manners too;
With shrewd but ever charitable ken
He read, and wrote out fair, the hearts of men;
Yet, in self-knowledge vers'd, a sage outright,

His giant soul was humble in its might!
O gentle, happy, modest mind,
O genial, cheerful, frank and kind,
Not even could domestic strife
Sour the sweetness of thy life,—
But wheresoe'er thy foot might roam,
Divorced from that Xantipp'd home,
Friends ever found thee,— ay, and foes,
Cordial to these, and kind to those;
Brave, loving, patient, generous, just, and good,—
Beloved by all, our matchless Shakspeare stood!

VI.
Where are thy glorious works unknown?
Who hath not heard thy fame?
On every shore, in every zone,
The World, with glad acclaim,
Yea, from the cottage to the throne,
Hath magnified thy name!
From far Australia to Vancouver's pines,
From the High Alps to Russia's deepest mines,
From China, with her English lesson learnt,
To Chili, wailing for her daughters burnt;
There, everywhere, our Shakspeare breathes and moves
In the sweet ether of all human loves!—
Where rent America now writhes in woe,
Where Nile and Danube, Thames and Ganges flow,
Wherever England sails, and human kind
Anywhere feels in heart, and thinks in mind,
There, everywhere, our Shakspeare's voice is heard,
By him all souls are thrill'd, and cheer'd, and stirr'd;
Each passion flows or ebbs, as Shakspeare speaks,
Hate knits the brow, or terror pales the cheeks,
Love lights the eyes, or pity melts the heart,
And all men bow beneath our Poet's art!

VII.
What monument to rear,
What worthy offering?—
Nought lacks thy glory here
Of all thy sons can bring:
Long since, a twin-sphered brother spake,
How vain it were to raise
To such a Name, for Memory's sake,
Its pyramid of praise:
Our Shakspeare needs no sculptured stones,
No temple for his honoured bones!
But haply in his native street
Beside the rescued home
Hallowed by his infant feet
Whereto all pilgrims roam,

A College well might rear its head,
That Townsman's name to bear,
And brother-actors' sons he bred
To light and learning there!
And, for great London and its throngs,—
To Shakspeare of old right belongs
The Shakspeare Bridge, with Shakspeare scenes
Sculptured upon its pannell'd screens,
Colossus-like the Thames to span,
And telling every passing man
Where a poor player in his youth
Served Heaven and Earth by mimic truth,
And wrapped in Art's and Nature's robe,
Leased,— 'twas his Heritage, — the Globe!—

VIII.
Great Magician for all time,
Denizen of every clime,
Darling poet of mankind,
Master of the human mind,
Nature's very priest and king,—
Take the gifts thy children bring!
Let thy Spirit, hovering o'er
Thine earthly home and haunts of yore,
In its wisdom, wealth, and worth,
Shine upon us from above,
While thy kinsmen here on earth
Thus with pious care and love
Celebrate our Shakspeare's birth.

On The Site of A Mulberry-Tree; Planted By Wm. Shakspeare; Felled By The Rev. F. Gastrell by Dante Gabriel Rossetti

This tree, here fall'n, no common birth or death
Shared with its kind. The world's enfranchised son,
Who found the trees of Life and Knowledge one,
Here set it, frailer than his laurel-wreath.
Shall not the wretch whose hand it fell beneath
Rank also singly—the supreme unhung?
Lo! Sheppard, Turpin, pleading with black tongue
This viler thief's unsuffocated breath!
We'll search thy glossary, Shakspeare! whence almost,
And whence alone, some name shall be reveal'd
For this deaf drudge, to whom no length of ears
Sufficed to catch the music of the spheres;
Whose soul is carrion now,—too mean to yield
Some Starveling's ninth allotment of a ghost.

www.ingramcontent.com/pod-product-compliance
Lightning Source LLC
Chambersburg PA
CBHW071508040426
42444CB00008B/1549